Praise for

"I've had the good fortune to be Carlo's friend and fan for several years. In *AfterLIFE* he shares his incredible journey to finding more of what his life's purpose is all about. His honest vulnerability and hard-but-beautiful-lessons learned will serve open-minded readers well. Like any good improviser, writer, or human, Carlo shares his story to help others. I always leave a conversation with Carlo feeling lucky, and I feel even luckier to have his wisdom in print to turn to anytime I need a quick injection of it."

~ **KEVIN MCKERNAN**, FOUNDER, THE IMPROV SHOP

"Carlo has tapped into the very deep questions we all face on a daily basis but always seem to set aside to be pondered some day in the future. In sharing his own experiences, he offers a new way, a new life—if we are willing to listen to the whispers in the wind. But his message is not just about hearing those whispers but also stepping off the cliff of our comfortable lives and having the courage it will take. I strongly recommend this book to anyone searching for a life of true meaning. You will not be disappointed."

~ **JACK DAVIS**, ENTREPRENEUR

"Carlo's epiphany and life transformation shines a light for us all. If you are low in joy and high in frustration or stress, you are not living your ideal life. Reading *AfterLIFE* will provide insight and maybe even a compass-like direction that leads to living a fulfilling life."

~ **DAN DAVIS**, CFP®
PRESIDENT & CO-FOUNDER, ADK WEALTH ADVISORY GROUP

"*AfterLIFE* starts off feeling like a simple and sweet read, and by the time you finish this book, you'll realize Carlo's journey has changed you. I laughed out loud several times, but more importantly, I found myself on a personal journey into my inner being where I reflected on Carlo's words and was transformed and changed by them."

~ **ALI TATARYN**, ARTIST, COACH, FACILITATOR

"Anyone going through times of question, reflection, and yearning for growth should pick up Carlo's book. His accounts of his own 'becoming' are shared with exuberance and truth and are relatable. His struggles and victories inspire the reader to look within and discover their own areas calling for attention and growth."

~ **JILL DUNCAN**, FARMHER AT LOVING ROOTS URBAN FARM
AND BODYWORKER AT WELLNESS BY JILL

"Love, empathy, and forgiveness are gifts so readily given to others, yet these same gifts are met with extraordinary resistance when reserved for ourselves. The thought of self-affirming change can be a mental hurdle so towering that we refuse to even try. This book is a testament to trusting your own heart, and undeniable proof that "love for yourself" is truly love's high-water mark. Carlo illustrates how he found his path back to an authentic life in a way that is both relatable and profound. True to his character, Carlo communicates important lessons he learned with brevity, kindness, and plainspoken sincerity.

Think of this book as a traveler's guide for your own journey. A roadmap that you can use to glean principles to defeat the bullies of fear and self-doubt when they block your trail. There is no blueprint for a happy life, but I believe success leaves clues. That's what Carlo offers in this book—clues. Those clues come in the form of the author's honest vulnerability, oak-like integrity, and an unflinching willingness to risk with confidence. Gather up the clues you find useful and apply them to your own life and maybe you, too, can wake up from your American dream."

~ **RAFE WILLIAMS**, MEDIA MAGNATE AND COMEDY GURU

"Carlo Sanfilippo understands that the practice of vulnerability is equal parts challenging and liberating. It's not an easy thing to commit to sincere individuality in a career field or culture where everyone is expected to conform. But Carlo leads by example and shares his life's tips in this affirming and inspirational story. He's not trying to be a hero or modern 'influencer,' but writes genuinely and gracefully. He encourages all of us, regardless of experience, age, income or number of degrees, to say yes to the things that inspire us, for indeed, it is those moments of 'yes' that can improve our lives forever. As a professional artist, I appreciate Carlo's encouragement to follow our instincts and the consistent push toward exploration as a never-ending, daily journey."

~ **CHELSEA RITTER-SORONEN**, ARTIST

"The journey of unbecoming of who we thought we should be to become who we want to be, it is universal and relevant. Carlo's enthusiasm and curiosity and his witty writing will awaken your creativity and open the windows to your heart.
Danke Danke Danke!"

~ **ELLI RICHTER**, INTEGRATIVE SUBCONSCIOUS COACH

After
LIFE

CARLO PIETRO SANFILIPPO

After LIFE

Waking Up from
My American Dream

Stonebrook Publishing
Saint Louis, Missouri

STONEBROOK
PUBLISHING

A STONEBROOK PUBLISHING BOOK
©2021 Carlo Pietro Sanfilippo

This book was guided in development and
edited by Nancy L. Erickson, The Book Professor®
TheBookProfessor.com

Library of Congress Control Number: 2020921835
ISBN: 978-1-7358021-2-1

www.stonebrookpublishing.net
PRINTED IN THE UNITED STATES OF AMERICA
10 9 8 7 6 5 4 3 2 1

Dedication

*This book is for my sons,
who've come with me on this journey
with love and patience.*

Table of CONTENTS

INTRODUCTION

> *We must be willing to let go of the life*
> *we planned so as to have the life*
> *that is waiting for us.*
>
> ~ JOSEPH CAMPBELL

HERE **WE ARE**. You and I. Millions of thoughts, decisions, and actions have brought me to the point of sharing my story with you, just as you've experienced many thoughts, decision, and actions before arriving here with this book in your hands.

My story is about leaving behind a prescribed lifestyle and learning to trust myself, to love myself, and to listen to that voice that had whispered my dreams to me for so long. Dreams that felt like a forever away, *some day*, always on the horizon, never getting any closer. Then in a blink of an eye, my world was shaken in a way I could never have imagined. Nearly a decade has passed since then, and I still feel that magnificent impact.

This is a book about transition and becoming, about learning to live intentionally, about living out loud and on purpose. It's about learning to live the life you want.

Far too many of us are on autopilot. At least I was for forty years, and it took immense pain for me to wake me up and change my focus. I'd worked hard and strived for all those years, but I wasn't chasing after or living *my own dream*. I was in a constant battle against myself, doing the things I thought were required of me, the things I thought I must. I was living according to a blueprint that had been handed to me and one that I accepted, but not one that I designed. I was constantly compromising and living a half-life—the life I thought I was supposed to live.

Ten years ago, I was living what many call the American Dream. I was married and living in a lovely home in a Norman Rockwellish-neighborhood. I had the things I thought I was supposed to have: a house, a mortgage, a couple of cars, two kids. All the things, all the stuff, and all the jobs and payments that go along with it. I was busy, busy, busy earning a living *but not living my life*. Earning money and then sending it off in bits and pieces to everyone else. When I wasn't earning money, I spent my time taking care of all the things we had or making plans to accumulate still more things. In between, I tried to be the best dad I could be.

Then life changed in an instant. Within four years I lost my mom, my stepfather, my dad, my marriage, and the whole way of life I'd spent my twenties and thirties building.

That unimaginable pain broke me down until I stopped fighting myself because, as you'll see, I was the one who'd held myself back. I was my harshest critic, my own worst enemy. Even though I'd found a million reasons to blame other people for my life, it had always been me doing it to myself: me hushing my own dreams, me holding myself back, me doubting my ideas, and me keeping me from the life I wanted. Once I learned to listen to and follow those whispers, my life began to change.

As I moved forward, I stumbled upon many tools and people who helped me along the way. The things I learned and the changes I made weren't the result of any single event or from reading a specific book, and they certainly weren't due to anyone else. I simply attracted and built a world based on what was inside of me.

But before I got there, the tempest nearly broke me. My suffering eventually forced me let go. I finally stopped struggling. As I stepped onto a new path, I found plenty of people whose love, words, and actions helped me move forward.

Now I want to share these lessons with you—and anyone—who feels the whisper of longing to live a different way. To follow your dream. To follow a path where you progressively realize your dreams and ideals. I will share the things that lit me up, in hopes of lighting the way for you.

Sound good? Then come with me and maybe, just maybe, bits and pieces of my story will inspire you to trust and love yourself enough to say *yes* to that whisper. To say *yes* to your dreams, so you can build the life you want one step at a time.

It's not easy, but it is simple.

Chapter
ONE

Trust Yourself

As soon as you trust yourself,
you will know how to live.
~ JOHANN WOLFGANG VON GOETHE

AS I MADE MY WAY through the winter of my life—the time when my parents died and I got divorced—I hired a life coach. An amazing person. Her name is Elli. I'd never done anything like that before, but I was having trouble finding my direction, and I needed help. I didn't realize that I was struggling so much because my options were now wide open, when they'd always felt ordered and prescribed. I wanted this coach to give me an action plan, but I came out of it with something else altogether.

Everything in my upbringing had either quietly or overtly reinforced that I had problems to solve, and the solutions involved pleasing others. There was so much pressure to be, have, and do certain things by a prescribed age. There was so much stuff I thought I had to own to show my family, friends, and the world that I mattered, that I was doing it—whatever *it* was—and that I was smart and good.

I'd always been good at figuring out a plan for myself if I knew what outcome I wanted. Growing up, my plan was to get through school. Then it was to figure out college. Then it was marriage and everything that came after that.

When I was only twenty-four, I was married and had a son, and after that all kinds of structures were laid out for me: get a house, start a career, make money, send money to all the bill collectors, be a dad, buy more things, fix the things, clean the things. There wasn't much freedom and few options in any of these scenarios, especially because I was married and always had to consider someone else. At least that's what I accepted as truth.

Further, I was in a career that had a precise image I felt I needed to maintain. I'd ask myself, *How should a financial planner look? How should I dress? What kind of car should I have? Where should I live?* I didn't feel freedom in any of these areas, only allegiance to the image. The things I did and the choices I made didn't bring me joy because they weren't coming from inside me.

So, after the divorce, my coach—Elli—and I went through several sessions where I looked backward and then dreamed forward.

One day she said, "Carlo, you need to learn to be your own best friend. You need to learn to have your back. To be whole."

"What?!" I said. My gut reaction was so strong that I felt an actual jolt. Was what she suggested even possible or acceptable? I was so conditioned to not value myself that her statement felt like heresy.

Becoming my own best friend was contrary to my entire upbringing. Through some combination of nature and nurture, there wasn't even a chance of me listening to myself. Growing up Catholic, I was told that God was watching me and when He wasn't, Santa certainly was. I was under the constant supervision and critique of the adults in my life. Be my own best friend?! Pfft.

But another part of me was curious. That part wanted to learn how to do this because I knew how long I'd been ignoring my own instincts and the price I'd paid for it in terms of life, happiness, and stress. The right combination of situations and information came at just the right time to allow big insights and change.

During this time, I'd also been doing quite a bit of shadow work (I'll talk more about that later) and through that, I'd noticed something myself: I did not speak my truth. From lots of contemplation and journaling, I became more and more aware of how I hadn't honored my truth. I often didn't trust myself or my own instincts, though they'd been whispering to me for years. I simply hadn't been willing to listen.

How Art Helped Me Learn to Trust Myself

After the divorce, I moved into a condominium. In the beginning, I had a mattress on the floor and ate my meals on a card table and folding chairs that my brother and sister-in-law, Mark and Jamie, had loaned me. One night while we were having dinner at their house, Jamie asked how my search for new furniture was going. I actually hadn't put much thought or energy into it.

Like many men I knew, I hadn't had much input into how our home had been decorated, even though I'd lived there for fifteen years. I'd never picked out a piece of furniture by myself. Or art, or a dish, or towels, sheets, blankets, wall color, carpet—nothing. Suddenly all of that was on me. On me. That's how it felt initially, but eventually it felt liberating and amazing.

Jamie said, "You need to find your style."

I had no idea what she was talking about, so I started to think about it. Over the course of the next few weeks, I looked online, in catalogs, and roamed around some stores wondering, *What is my style?*

A few weeks later, the question came up again. By then, I'd looked around enough to know that I liked the style of furniture at Restoration Hardware. I love history and the imperfections of the materials that had been repurposed from their original design was fascinating to me. The dings and scratches told stories, stories my pain could relate to. But I also felt defeated and annoyed; the dining table I liked cost $10,000.

"It's just made out of old flooring and lumber," I told Jamie. "Why does it cost $10,000? That's silly. I could make it for far less."

"You should!" she quickly answered. "You totally could make a table."

Again, I had something to contemplate. Could I make a table? Go find old things and put them together to make my own table? Maybe I could.

A seed was planted, and the idea grew. Over the next few weeks, I looked more closely at tables and furniture that I liked. I looked in stores, on the web, in books—as many places as I could. Then I jumped online and tried to find sources of old flooring. My first Google search led me to a place in the city that became my "Room of Requirement," like what Harry Potter had at Hogwarts.

I called the guy, Reagan, who had a gigantic warehouse of salvaged materials. I told him what I was looking for, and he encouraged me to come by. He took me to a pile of maple hardwood flooring that he'd rescued from a warehouse that was torn down. I picked through it until I had what I wanted. Then I looked around a bit more and stumbled across a dirty, beat up fireplace mantle. I asked him how much it cost, and he pointed me to a wall with other ones he thought were in better shape. After looking at those, I decided I liked the first one best.

"It's a 120-year-old mantle that I rescued from an old drug store that was being demolished," he said, "but it's in pretty rough shape. Why do you want that one?"

I explained my idea for making it into an entertainment center for my TV. And that's when Reagan became my art therapist. I hadn't realized the creativity and talent this man possessed. The reason he collected all these orphaned things was because he liked to make things too. He could see the stories the old things told, and he wanted to preserve them.

Reagan grabbed a yellow pad and a black marker and sketched a few suggestions to make my idea work. He took me back to his workshop and showed me the right stain to buy, so I could match the color of my new shelving to the original stain. For a few extra dollars, he added some boards to make the mantel deep enough to be a shelf and a bit taller to be at the right viewing height. He even helped me get it home and up three flights of stairs on my fire escape.

Using the sketch that Reagan made and the tools I'd acquired over the years when I'd rehabbed our one hundred-year-old house, I got to work. As I bought, cut, sanded, and stained lumber, removed old paint, added shelves and lighting, the old fireplace was slowly transformed.

I didn't actually know how it would turn out, but that didn't matter. The project revealed itself to me as I went along. I'd left old paint on it that somehow complimented the stained wood. Some parts didn't blend in the way I wanted, so I went to an art store and bought some red and black oil paints and added and blended colors until it looked right to me. To *me*. I was the audience.

That was my revelation. I wasn't putting together a puzzle that had to look a certain way. This wasn't a piece of Ikea furniture. Each piece and part of it was finished when it looked right *to me*. It was finished when it served the function that I needed. When I liked it.

Nearly everything I'd done before this had been done with another set of eyes—actual or metaphorical—on me. How I dressed, what my hair looked like, what I studied in college, how I spent my money. But this was different. This project was for me alone, and it would be finished when I was satisfied. I began to see how the structure and system I'd always lived under had depended on me not trusting myself, my opinions, my likes and dislikes.

Covered in sawdust, with paint and stain on my hands and clothes, I had a revelation: if I was going to become my own best friend, I had to trust myself, and this process felt good. Because I was learning to trust what I liked, this project was fun and easy. I felt a flow and energy that was exhilarating.

> *This project was for me alone, and it would be finished when I was satisfied.*

Trust is vital in any relationship, but my upbringing and society itself had taught me to trust others but not myself. It actually felt more like obeying others rather than trusting them. *Just do what you're told and don't question.* I was conditioned to ignore my own instincts, which led me into unhealthy relationships that reinforced the notion that my ideas were no good, my instincts were wrong, my taste was bad, my jokes were dumb.

I believed this about myself and often prefaced an idea with, "This is how my dumb brain thinks." I said this a lot and still catch myself sometimes. And when I hear those words coming from others, my heart breaks a little because I recognize myself in them.

When my sons came over to my condo for the week, they saw the six-foot-tall mantle that rested on sawhorses in the center of my living room. Of course, it was in the middle of the room; I hadn't bought a couch or any other furniture yet. My tools were spread out across the floor because I'd essentially turned the living room into my workshop. They stopped and stared.

"Uh, what's that, Dad?"

"We're going to put the TV in there," I told the boys. "I'm turning it into an entertainment center."

This was a new experience and journey for me, so it was certainly new and odd for them. But my sons began to get a glimpse of the Carlo that had been asleep for too long.

Week after week, as the mantle unfolded into what I wanted to create, the boys could finally see my vision, and they got excited. The top part of the mantle had a big opening where there had once been a mirror. I envisioned putting some kind of artwork there but wasn't sure what would work. My lifelong love of art had been rekindled. At this point my entire home was my canvas, and as time went on the color spread into the rest of my life.

"It'd be cool if we put an aquarium there," my older son Alex said.

In my mind's eye I could see the glow of an aquarium and the color and life it would bring to our space. I agreed that it would work visually, but I thought that having a couple hundred gallons of water above our electronics on the third floor of a condo probably wouldn't be wise. I was also on a drive to simplify my life, and a fish tank represented lots of chores and complications, which I didn't want.

I let my imagination work on this concept for a while. One night, from the vantage point of my borrowed card table and folding chair, I sat and stared at that space while I ate my super-bachelor meal that included a Heineken and a Trader Joe's three-cheese pizza generously seasoned with green Tabasco®.

I thought about how much my sons and I liked fossils. I had a vision of fish fossils swimming around in that space. I went back to the web and within minutes, I found a fossil dealer. I ordered nine rectangular slate blocks that had really cool fish fossils on them. When they arrived, I mounted them to a metal backing with magnets and arranged them in a square to symbolize the nine dots from the lesson about thinking outside the box. I had made the art that I wanted, and we got the fish my son wanted.

I felt a rush of excitement about what else might be possible. I had tasted a sense of trust in myself and freedom that launched me on a new journey. I still have my four-million-plus-year-old fish to remind me of this lesson.

After I finished the fireplace, I built a coffee table from a crate that had been constructed in 1899. I built my own four-poster bed from old porch posts and stair railings. And then I finally made my dining room table from the maple flooring I'd bought from Reagan.

I learned that I had an artistic side that I'd ignored since high school. I had enjoyed art, but because I compared myself to others, I didn't think I was good enough. So, I didn't pursue it beyond my classes.

> **I learned that I had an artistic side that I'd ignored since high school.**

I also learned something from the comments my friends and neighbors made about my woodworking. I felt the powerful and persistent pressure from people and society about who I was—or rather, who they thought I should be. We're so often defined by what we do for work and how we do it that deviating from those confines can upset or confuse others. My new neighbors, for example.

The building I'd moved into was built in the 1920s. At one point, it had been apartments but was later abandoned and then rehabbed into condos in 2008. I live in a three-story tower of six units but, at first, I had only three neighbors because all the condos weren't yet sold. Because the building wasn't fully occupied, the basement/storage area below our units was pretty empty. So, I threw together a makeshift workshop down there and worked on my projects here and there between my responsibilities as a father and business owner. I met many of my neighbors as they passed through the area, and we struck up numerous conversations. They'd often ask what I did for a living, and when I told them I had a financial planning practice, they were shocked.

"What? I thought you were a carpenter!" I laughed at this.

"How can you do all these things if you're a financial planner? You're a numbers guy!" they'd say.

And people who knew me from before I started this new hobby were equally shocked and sometimes a little uncomfortable. My friends were blown away that I could make things. I heard so many disbelieving comments.

"You just, like, made a table?" Whoa! Are you going to be a carpenter now?"

"I thought you were a financial planner. Are you starting a new business?

"Are you quitting your practice?"

"What are you doing? Who are you?"

The old Carlo would've been troubled by all of this. He would've picked up on their distress and sought to self-edit. Instead, I saw that the stress and discomfort was theirs, not mine. I could now trust what I liked and wanted, and that gave me a profound sense of calm and peace. Sure, I was doing this new thing, but this thing wasn't me. It was fun, it made me happy, it challenged me, and it helped me heal and grow. I was beginning to have my own back, and I didn't let anyone else shape my feelings or actions.

Later, I visited Reagan and his Room of Requirement again to search for something I needed for my next project. He always knew where I could find what I needed, and he joked that he'd become my art therapist. He was more right than he knew—or more right than I knew at that moment. Using my imagination and creativity to build the core things in my home was an amazingly important step in learning to trust myself. I'd gone off script for the first time in my life, and it worked. I felt more alive than I had in years.

Other than my trips to see Reagan, this was an extremely solitary time. I spent hours and hours thinking about designs for my furniture—looking, reading, going to the library, wandering around furniture stores, hardware stores, bookstores, and the City Museum in Saint Louis.

I was partially drawn to these places for their artistic inspiration but also to remind myself that I didn't have to color inside the lines. If I wanted to build my own bed, I could. I could also make a table and all kinds of other things simply for the fun of it. I didn't have to change careers. I'd spent forty years trying to be what I thought others wanted, and now I was discovering what I wanted. I now understood what my coach, Elli, meant when she told me to be my own best friend.

Yes, I'd spent years living a prescribed life, but worse, I ignored the things that whispered to me. For example, when I was married, I kept getting ideas for a potting bench I wanted to make. I couldn't quite articulate the design, but I knew I'd make it from old things. And since I couldn't describe it, I could never quite sell my wife on the idea, so the project never came to life. Since I'd never done anything like that before, I didn't trust my instincts and didn't have the will to push it. It was only a potting bench; why didn't I just dive in and give it a try?

Instead, I started blaming others for the things I didn't do. I thought I needed outside permission but felt that no one believed in me. I continued blaming others for years, and it was an extremely difficult mindset to overcome. But when my deeply personal and creative projects that I built during my solitary time turned out better than I imagined, I gained the strength and confidence to try other new things. I found out that the seeds of creativity and so much more had been inside me all along.

What's whispering to you? Try it! You aren't what you do. You aren't defined by your career, your age, or your roles. It doesn't matter if you're a father or mother, if you've reached a certain decade in life, or if no one else in your family or circle of friends has ever done it before. None of those things matter. Follow your curiosity. If playing an instrument keeps pulling at you, give it a try. Take a lesson, read a book, join a class, go to a Meetup—just try it.

It's been said that our outer world is a reflection of our inner world. Each affects the other, and if you change one, the other will be impacted. The radical changes in my thoughts and belief structure were about to spill over into the rest of my life.

Chapter TWO

Expand Trust and Love to Others

*No man is an island entire of itself;
every man is a piece of the continent,
a part of the main;*

~ JOHN DONNE, 1624

AS TIME PASSED, my condo started feeling like home. I had my dining room table that I'd made instead of my old, borrowed card table. I bought a couch to go in front of the entertainment center I made, and my mattress was on my new bed with a proper set of blankets and pillows to match. I was slowly building a space where I felt safe and inspired. I was beginning to heal from my divorce and the loss of my parents and was working hard to be the best father I could be. After all, my boys were experiencing these life changes too.

I finally lost my workshop space when all the condo units in my building were sold. I thought about renting a workshop, but I couldn't find anything close enough to home to be practical. And as gratifying as it had been to make all those things, I didn't want to turn my hobby into a business or a chore. The work was very solitary, which is what I needed at the time. I'd been sad back then, and I needed that time and space for myself. But now I wanted to do something else creative that involved other people. And that's exactly what found me.

When I didn't have an artistic outlet, I felt a bit adrift again. My life had been dominated by external structure for so long that I didn't know what to do with my free time. I was still healing and was often exhausted, and I found myself disappearing into video games for a while. It was my escape.

I felt like a part-time empty nester. My kids were with their mom half the time. For fifteen years I'd owned homes that always needed work. I'd completed the list of things I wanted to do to my condo. If there were no dust bunnies there were virtually no chores, and my Roomba took care of most of those! This feeling was so strange. I could do anything—but what? This new freedom was somehow uncomfortable.

I got lots of unsolicited advice about what to do and about "getting back out there." *Go meet people. Do online dating, join a Meetup group, go to a wine bar.* I tried some of those things like the wine bar. After my $45 meal and glass of wine, I was still hungry when I left, both physically and emotionally. It wasn't what I was looking for. I still had some healing, growth, and self-discovery ahead of me, so I went back to my video games.

One evening after work I was, yet again, at home on my couch slaying dragons, and my buddy Mike called.

"Hey! Why don't you come to an improv show with me tonight?" Mike asked. He was an enthusiastic performer and always wanted to build their audience.

He'd called me when I was married and had invited me to do things like this, but it wasn't an option in my old world. I was already conditioned to find excuses, and I was still depressed. My mind was already formulating an excuse when I had one of those out-of-body moments. I looked down at myself and realized that I was going to always be alone if I didn't get off that couch and start interacting with humans again. So, without even knowing what I was going to see, I went to my first show at a little bar in Saint Louis called The Tin Can.

I grabbed a beer and found a seat in that tiny bar/theater. It was a slow night, so I sat amongst the four other audience members and watched the actors do a thirty-minute long-form improvised set, all of which was inspired by a suggestion from the audience.

I was blown away by what I saw. On stage, there were ten or so people working together, making things up, creating characters, scenes, and worlds on the spot with an energy and a sense of fun and joy that I could feel. I didn't know what was happening or how they did it, but I was intrigued. I sat forward in my seat watching, laughing, and enjoying the trapeze act before my eyes.

Not long after that, Mike told me he was thinking about starting a workshop to teach improv. I was a bit hesitant to jump in, but he persisted, and he purposely scheduled the class around days when my kids were with their mom. As the first day of class approached, I found myself looking for excuses, but in the end, I said yes and went. Soon I was participating in weekly workshops and having a blast.

A year later, again at Mike's suggestion, I enrolled in long-form classes at the Improv Shop, diving into an art form that I hadn't known existed just a year ago. A year after that, I successfully auditioned for a house team at The Improv Shop (a Harold team for any fellow improv nerds who may be reading), and I've performed with them now for nearly five years.

So, what is this improv thing and why do I dig it so much?

While doing improv, I experienced the same fun of having a creative outlet that I did when making furniture, but now it had the added benefit of a social element. I'm certain I wouldn't have been ready for improv if I hadn't rediscovered my creativity, my voice—and most importantly—learned to trust myself while making my furniture. To jump into a class with strangers and make up characters, dialogue, emotions, and situations meant that I had to trust myself.

Improv is a supreme act of vulnerability and an exercise in trust. You jump into characters, scenes, emotions, and situations in front of an audience. You perform a show only once and then it's over, never to be performed again. It's all unscripted and free— quite unlike my old life.

I learned and practiced skills but not lines, characters, or situations. I had to focus on listening to what was said, watching how it was said, observing my scene partner's body language, what details my teammates added from the sidelines, what landed with the audience, and what emotions I felt. And then I learned to respond as genuinely as I could from all those cues. Both in practice and in shows, I learned to respond freely and intuitively over and over again.

One of the coaches encouraged us to let our emotions lead our characters to responses that come from a more genuine place, as opposed to looking for an intellectual or clever response. We were searching for the humor in life and relationships.

That was the polar opposite of what I'd done for so long. External pressures and forces had always driven me, not what was inside. Not what I wanted. Not what whispered to me. This art form helped me tap into listening to and trusting what came up inside me. In the process, I was becoming more sure of my own inner voice and more open to my off-stage choices in my life. Plus, there was the added benefit of working with other people with whom I could be vulnerable and trust.

> ### *This art form helped me tap into listening to and trusting what came up inside me.*

I really learned the point after graduation. During one of our first practices for the house team I'd joined, our teacher addressed us.

"If you all are going to be successful, you're going to learn to love and trust each other."

That felt strange to me. I politely listened but didn't fully understand what he meant, nor did I believe it.

Over time, I figured it out. We went on stage in front of audiences again and again, making up thirty-minute shows from a simple audience suggestion without any scripted lines, costumes, props, or anything. We had to deconstruct the suggestion and turn that raw material into something entertaining and sometimes very meaningful. In order to do so, we had to trust ourselves and our team.

It was a lot like mental and emotional skydiving. I'd step into a scene with a specific idea, but if my scene partner initiated the scene, they'd take me in a very different direction. So, I'd have to drop my idea and dive into supporting my partner. And they did the same for me. To develop this kind of trust in people, to know that I could leap into something and my friends would catch me, was an amazing feeling. We trusted each other and loved each other.

And the more I did this on stage, the easier it was to do off stage. Just like I didn't start making furniture to have an epiphany or to accelerate my personal growth, I was now learning about the relationship between trust and love from this amazing art form. More walls came down that allowed me to see my truth, to speak it, and to act on it. Just a few years earlier, I couldn't have done this. I hadn't trusted myself, so I certainly wouldn't have trusted another person enough to get on stage and step into this scary world.

There was another benefit of improv. Now that I'd found a tribe of people who enjoyed laughing, being silly, having fun, and supporting each other, for the first time in a long time, I felt accepted. Simple things like laughter and having fun had once come easily for me, but when I entered the adult world and bought a car, bought a house, went to work to pay for that house, spent my weekends taking care of and fixing the house—and being a dad in between all of that—I lost the playfulness I'd had as a kid.

One day after one of my first workshops, I was feeling very happy and content because of some positive notes the teacher had given me. Somewhere on my drive home, I realized that I was having fun because I was just letting loose and being myself. After years of not trusting myself, not loving myself, not having my back, and not being my own best friend, I'd learned not to respect myself, which had led to so many unfulfilling relationships, interactions, and situations. I had constantly edited my words to what I thought I should say or do, and I wasn't being myself. This accidental discovery of another new passion opened my mind to the fact that I had the freedom to create my own world.

I was alone in the sense of not having a partner, but I wasn't really alone. Alone but not lonely. I'd first heard that from a friend who filled her time with triathlons and distance running. One day I complimented her on all the things she was engaged in and she explained that she was *alone but not lonely*. Pursuing her own passions and growth fulfilled her. That sounded amazing to me, and it made more and more sense in the years that followed.

Radical Love

It's easy for me to see how I've learned and grown as a result of embracing these art forms. The quiet solitude of making things that are beautiful and useful taught me to trust my taste, my opinions, and my judgement. Stepping into a community of loving, creative, supportive, and trusting people gave me permission to be myself, which really set me free. Even though this was practiced in a group setting, it reinforced what my life coach, Elli, had tried to teach me a few years prior. That what I sought in others was *in me*. That I am lovable. That in trusting myself, I can take steps toward really loving myself. And from that place of love and trust, I've taken so many more positive, powerful, and brave steps that I would not have taken otherwise.

You know what really blew me away? A few years into this part of my journey, I was walking through a park and I had an overwhelming feeling of being in love—but I wasn't dating anyone. I was taken aback because this feeling wasn't about me or some other person; it was simply a state of love that permeated everything. I'd known this feeling other times in life, but it had always been a love for someone—someone outside of me that I needed to feel fulfilled. I didn't fight it because it felt wonderful. I realized that my capacity to love was growing. Quite the opposite of my original opinion that self-love equaled narcissism. The feeling transcended my individual self quite entirely.

Chapter
THREE

Rippling Changes

It is good to love many things,
for therein lies the true strength,
and whosoever loves much performs
much, and can accomplish much,
and what is done in love is well done.

~ VINCENT VAN GOGH

ONE OF THE MOST SURPRISING and rewarding—
and for the old Carlo, counterintuitive—results of learning
to trust and love myself was that I became a better father. I loved
my boys with all my heart before and after the changes in me, but
in my old life, I couldn't show up as my truest self with them and
for them. But when I learned how to be honest and vulnerable
with myself, I became fully honest and vulnerable with them.

It's a valuable lesson that applies to every type of relationship you have, not just the parent-child relationship. As a result of
many conversations I've had with my clients about the changes I'd
made—conversations I never would have had in my old life—some
of them have made changes in their own lives. And my friends and

family have also been inspired because of what they witnessed in me. We're all a part of the systems that surround us, and when one person changes, everyone is affected.

Here's a bit of my story for the people nearest and dearest to me. I have two nearly grown boys that I've loved with all my heart since the day they were born. I don't have any "Cats in the Cradle" regrets. I've always made time for them, and I've been fortunate to be in control of my calendar since I started my career. I've been there for camping trips, hikes, various practices and shows, school plays, concerts, parent-teacher meetings, and so much more. But even though I was there, I wasn't whole because I didn't know how to be honest with myself. Since I didn't trust and love myself, I couldn't show up as my best self. Thus, I was modeling an archetype I didn't like that my sons would likely repeat.

> ### *I was modeling an archetype I didn't like that my sons would likely repeat.*

If anyone had told me this, it would've broken my heart. In fact, a few people did just that. Right before my divorce, I was having a drink and talk with my brother. I was going through a tremendous amount of pain and suffering as I tried to decide what to do. I'd convinced myself that I couldn't get divorced because of the devastating experience I'd had growing up with divorced parents.

My father left us when I was five, and I barely saw him after that. He died not that many years ago, and I barely knew him. That left a scar that I'm still healing from. Some people will conform to and replicate the archetype that was modeled for them by their parents; others carry it around like a boogey man. I did the latter. I was so determined not to cause my boys the same anguish that I ended up as a father who was *there* but not *whole*. I was fighting the shadow of "not being my father" and that kept me from being the father I could be.

The tremendous amount of stress and mental energy I wasted in not being my dad kept be from just being me. I didn't see or understand it, but my brother gently said, "You're not yourself in your marriage, Carlo."

Hearing that was like being in a deep, deep dream state when someone in real life calls your name. I heard and understood what he said, but it sounded distant and almost foreign, like I was deep in the netherworld. I continued on with my life after that but didn't know what to do with this new truth. It was a crisis.

Soon after, I started seeing a therapist for the first time in my life. I finally broke down and asked for help. I was deeply unhappy and didn't know what to do. My stepdad had just passed away, and he was the closest person I'd had to a father. I thought he would live to be one hundred, but a brain tumor swept him away in a very short time in his early seventies.

While I waited for my first session, a door opened, and one of the staff members walked across the room. I thought, *God, please don't let that be her.* I knew from a glance that she couldn't understand me. Couldn't understand my pain.

I found out in forty-five minutes how wrong I was.

During that session, I laid out my situation and all my misery and said something I'd been thinking for many years.

"It's only ten more years," I told her.

It turns out that my therapist was an amazing woman who I guessed was between seventy and seventy-five years old. She was like the wisest tribal leader a person could hope for—the perfect person to be in my life in that moment, which was ironic given my original and inaccurate prejudgment.

After I said, "only ten more years" she gave me a peculiar look. She wasn't looking at me but, rather, I could feel her looking into me. I could feel her years of wisdom and experience peering into me with kindness tinged with sadness.

"Ten more years?" she asked.

"Yes, in ten more years then Graham will be eighteen and I can get divorced.

She leaned in and said, "Carlo, you're too young to write off a decade of your life."

Bah! What did she know!? I could feel my walls coming up to block this out. To give her the litany of arguments I had given myself so many years. I can't get a divorce. I can't be my father! I can't give up. I can't be a sinner. I can't have that label. I can't be weak. I can't quit . . . but I felt like I had no other choice. My guard was down because of the stress I was under, and I could hear the truth in what she said. I didn't have the energy to fight it.

And yet, my rational mind quickly countered that I had to be there for my boys. I couldn't leave them. I couldn't be a bad dad. I would *not* be my father. All my old ghosts came flooding forward to defend my pain, to keep me trapped in my situation.

I wasn't angry; I was defensive. I had to defend my pain. I had to justify my sacrifice. It was for them. I had to stay in this painful situation to be a good father, didn't I?

"Carlo," she said, "you're teaching your boys an archetype. You're teaching them that how you live, how you act, what you do, is normal. They will likely recreate that same dynamic in their own relationships and in their own families because they're growing up thinking it's normal. You aren't letting them get to know you. They only see this version of you that's barely surviving."

OOF! Pow! Bang! I felt like a criminal in an old Batman comic. It was like a punch to the gut. My therapist wasn't trying hurt me, but with her gentle words, she'd held up a mirror and I saw my situation very clearly. I thought about that and what my brother had said to me, and I finally became aware of my hard truth. This was my pivotal moment, and it ushered me into a time of introspection and growth.

I eventually started working with my life coach, Elli, who suggested that I should/could love myself and be my own best friend. As I rediscovered parts of myself that had been dormant, my sons discovered a side of me they'd never seen before. I was still there for them, but now I was different. I was not only building and creating things, but a more complete version of me was emerging. I was learning new things. My experience with art through building furniture and my improv performances demonstrated to my boys that we aren't what we do.

> *As I rediscovered parts of myself that had been dormant, my sons discovered a side of me they'd never seen before.*

They saw me start with small ideas—ideas I couldn't fully explain to anyone. I had only vague concepts of what I was looking for and what I wanted to create. Sometimes the boys went exploring with me to some of the salvage places I'd discovered. I took them to my Room of Requirement and let them roam around. They met Reagan, and he gave them each an iron star from an old nineteenth century brick building, which had been part of the structure that held it together. In the process, we learned a bit more about the functional architecture of the buildings all around us in our city. They saw me transform the mantel I'd found there into our entertainment center, and they saw me transform an 1899 crate—that we'd used to hold shovels in our garage—into our new coffee table. They watched me take piles of lumber and turn them into our dining room table, where we now eat. Then they watched me on stage with new friends being playful, joyful, and creative.

When I was their age, my mom had instilled in me a love for the natural world. When I was in the process of unpacking and decorating my new home, I opened a shoe box and found a piece of petrified wood that she'd given me in grade school. I'd kept that rock on my desk from grade school until after college. But after I was married, it ended up in a shoe box of my stuff; it didn't fit in with the décor of our family home.

As I held this golf-ball-sized rock in my hands, years of memories flooded my mind of my mom bringing it back from California, of holding it and pondering it at my childhood desk, studying it and daydreaming though time, imagining when it was a piece of a living tree. Holding this gift from my mom that had been hidden away for years—like the real me had been—I realized that I was as interested in nature and natural science as I had been back then.

I put the rock on our breakfast bar because I wanted it in my space once again. A few days later when the boys were over, eight-year-old Graham reached his tiny hand up to the breakfast bar, grabbed it, and said, "What's this Dad"?

"What do you think it is?" I asked.

"A rock! A piece of wood! Both?!"

The excitement and curiosity in his face lit me up, and we fell into a great conversation about fossilization of this ancient tree, how minerals can leach into the cells of organic matter and slowly transform them into stone. Pulling this rock out of a dark shoe box and bringing into the light of day was exactly what was happening to me. The joy and excitement I had with my son that day, and have had with both boys over the years, washed away any shred of doubt I had about my decisions.

In fact, later that very year, we were having a drought in Missouri and we went to the confluence of the Mississippi and Missouri rivers. Because of the drought, we could walk more than one hundred yards into the dry riverbed. The exposed gravel bars were full of beautifully tumbled stones of granite, quartz, ancient tree amber, and all kinds of other rocks I didn't recognize. We'd heard that you could sometimes find bones and artifacts from the ice age.

I didn't expect to find anything like that but, sure enough, Graham came running to me with something curious. He held a bone that I didn't recognize. It was very dark brown and heavier than a bone should be. We guessed that it was in the process of becoming a fossil but not quite there yet. We had no idea what kind of animal it was from or what kind of bone it was.

The next day we went to the Saint Louis Science Center to see the paleontologists. We'd visited with them a few weeks earlier and had asked why we never found interesting bones in Missouri, only ancient marine life like coral, seashells, and crinoids. They explained that when the glaciers melted, they washed away the top layers of soil that, for the most part, had the fun dinosaur bones in them.

"But if you ever find anything interesting, bring it to us and we'll help identify it."

And now, less than a month later, we found something interesting. We got in line and waited our turn to speak with the scientist working that day. He took the bone from Graham.

"Hey, this is interesting," he said. "Where'd you find this? A gravel bar, I imagine."

He was absolutely right. Next, he turned it over a few times as Graham told him the story of his discovery.

He told us that it was an upper vertebrae of a baby bison from the ice age. From the weight and color, he estimated that it was between ten thousand to fifteen thousand years old. The look on Graham's face was priceless; I'll never forget it. He'd found a real treasure.

The next weekend we set out to my Room of Requirement. My goal was to find something that could serve as a shadow box for this treasure. We found what we were looking for, Graham printed a picture of a baby bison, wrote a small description, and hung it at eye level across from the toilet in his bathroom, so "people will have something interesting to look at while they're pooping." Priceless.

He was so proud of what he found, we learned so many things, we created fun memories, and he has a treasure. None of this would have happened with the old Carlo. The old me didn't have the space or drive to explore my passions, which kept those very things from my boys.

A seed had been planted that encouraged my kids to follow their curiosity and explore their imagination. And I'm convinced it was a result of me learning to be myself. Putting things in my home that I found interesting. Things that tell stories.

As I explored outside my old boundaries, I made new friends. We met Faring, a muralist whose artwork has been installed in cities around the USA and even in Europe. Another friend, Chelsea, a chalk artist, who went from being a part-time artist and working as a restaurant manager to having a full-time art business that does work all over the country and even in France and Australia. In my improv community, we've met many actors and comedians who have amazing futures ahead of them. I could go on and on describing the people I'm so proud of and inspired by.

As I was knee deep in these adventures and bringing my kids along with me as much as possible, something amazing started to happen. My sons started branching out themselves. My younger son, Graham, said "Dad, I think I want to learn to play piano." So, for Christmas I got him a keyboard and signed him up for piano lessons. One day while he was practicing, I heard him singing along. I asked him if he wanted to learn to sing, too, and he said yes. Before long he was singing in front of crowds of people at School of Rock concerts. As his confidence and creativity kept growing, the ideas kept rolling.

Around the same time my older son Alex, who was still in high school, decided to make a video game with his buddies. They collaborated through Skype and Dropbox, working remotely with one another that summer to self-learn programming in order to build their game. One day I woke at one o'clock in the morning and noticed the light was on in the dining room. I walked out to see what was going on and found Alex typing away at his computer. I asked him what he was doing, and he told me he had finally figured out the programing for turning the lights off and on in the house in his video game. He was busing rewiring this virtual house, so the lights worked! I was blown away at his focus and dedication to this project and the skills he'd learned on his own. Now he's taking computer science and math courses that are far, far beyond anything I understand about those subjects.

Not long after, the wheels started spinning for Graham and he said, "Dad, I think I want to make a video game too." I know nothing about programming, and I couldn't expect his sixteen-year-old brother to teach him. I knew Graham liked to draw and that he was inspired by all the artists we'd met, so we went to the art store and got a sketch pad and some colored pencils, so he could storyboard his ideas. That summer Graham took that sketch pad with him everywhere he went. Whenever he had a spare moment, he was doodling, drawing, and building his game. By the end of the summer he'd filled it up with a map of his world, including all the characters and the various scenes.

Then he told me he'd changed his mind. He wanted to write a book instead of making a video game. I had an old laptop that still worked, so Alex cleaned it up for him and off he went. Eighty thousand words later, and Graham had the first draft of a novel!

While I love my kids, this isn't meant to be about them or to brag. I can see that the actions they're taking and the passions they're following are a result of the freedom I've given myself to follow what inspires me. I learned to live on purpose. As a result, I built and created a new world for me *and* for them, where we all have permission to pursue our passions and try new things. And we stepped into the mix of other people who are doing the same—people who spend their lives creating.

As others inspired and motivated me, I took actions that were an example for my family and friends that gave them the courage to do the same. Others inspired me to love, trust, and accept myself, which showed my kids that they, too, could do new and interesting things, which then inspired me to the actions I'm taking at this very moment. For example, I never imagined I'd write a book, but watching my son knock out—at this point—two drafts of a story (he wrote a sequel to his first book because he felt he had more to say) inspired me to share my experiences.

Wherever you are in life, whether you have kids or don't, whether you're married or single, the life you live and the choices you make provide a living example and archetype for everyone else. The more action you take in the direction of your dreams, the more people you attract into your life whose path matches or complements your own. We are parts of a whole. When we heal and grow, it has an impact on the system we're part of, especially on those closest to us. As Gandhi said, we should "Be the change you want to see in the world."

And it feels effortless. I'm not trying to act a certain way. I'm just living my truth. Living on purpose.

Yes *and*

love is a place
& through this place of
love move
(with brightness of peace)
all places

yes is a world
& in this world of yes live
(skillfully curled)
all world

~ E.E. CUMMINGS

THERE'S A CONCEPT in improv called *"Yes and."* An entire long-form improv show is usually around thirty minutes or so, and we certainly don't have much time to build characters and plots. We have to dive right in and support each other. For example, if your scene partner says you're surfing in Hawaii, you say *yes and* add more facts about your feelings, relationship, and situation in order to build your world and the scene.

As I've gained more confidence in listening to and living my truth, my life has unfolded in ways I never imagined, even just a few years ago. Sometimes it feels like I'm just *Yes and*-ing my way through some really fun things in life.

When I was in high school—and later in college—I studied German. At first, I did it because I had to pick a language to fulfill my diploma and degree requirements. But then I went on an exchange trip in high school and had an amazing experience living with a family for a few weeks in Stuttgart, Germany. My time in Stuttgart transformed an abstract pile of grammar and vocabulary I'd been cramming into my head for quizzes and tests into a living, breathing language and culture that left an indelible mark on me.

Later in college, I participated in a work exchange program where I lived with a family and worked in a bank for the summer in a small town in Germany called Offenburg near the French border. At the time, I did these things because I thought they were practical—that learning a language and culture would "look good on my resume." I convinced myself that was why I spent eight years studying the language and culture of my maternal grandfather, Alvin.

After college, I started working as a financial planner. I was married, had a baby, and was building a career and all the pieces of the American Dream. With all my time and financial obligations, travel wasn't possible. With no near-term hope to travel, spending the time to learn another language felt like a waste of time. That part of my life was over. Stashed away in the shoe box with my fossils.

After my divorce, my sons and I started traveling a bit. At first, we did some road trips to see friends in other parts of the country. We drove to Santa Fe, New Mexico; we did another trip to Washington, DC; and we drove up and down the California coast. But in 2015, the thought popped in my head that I wanted to go back to Europe.

Why not? Why not pull this dream out of the shoe box? The prior few years had shown me how inexpensively the boys and I could travel, how well we traveled together, what good travelers they are, how travel expanded their understanding of the world and strengthened our relationship, and I learned that we genuinely like to do the same kinds of things.

So over dinner one night, I proposed the idea.

"Hey guys, would you like to go to Germany?" I asked.

"Yes!" they enthusiastically responded.

"And maybe we'll go to Austria too." I added.

I knew I had enough points from my credit card reward program to pay for the airline tickets, so the trip would be affordable. I began to do my research, and with the help of travel author Rick Steves, I built an itinerary. We would spend time in Munich, Germany, and the Austrian cities of Salzburg and Vienna. Because of Icelandic Air's policy at the time, we did a forty-eight-hour layover in and around Reykjavík, Iceland. I didn't even tell the boys about our layover until we were on the plane. It was so much fun.

Speaking with our Airbnb hosts, waiters and waitresses, museum staff and all sorts of locals, I was able to use my German again. I was thrilled and amazed at the vocabulary that flowed through from the recesses of my memory and out my mouth. I was super happy that locals would ask me where we were from, instead of guessing that we were Americans. They knew from my accent that we weren't natives, but it didn't tip them off that we were from the US. Many times, by the end of a meal, a waiter or waitress would finally ask where we were from. How did I know German? They dealt with tourists all the time who didn't know or wouldn't try to learn the basics.

It was so fun for me to use this skill that I'd spent eight years learning in my youth, and it was a delight to see my kids witness this part of me they hadn't known about. As I unpacked another piece of myself from the shoe box, I saw a look on their faces I'll always remember. More and more, they were seeing *me*.

During the trip, I was acutely aware of how happy I felt. How alive I felt from the mental stimulation of seeing so many things, diving so deep into the culture, art, history, and language of another land. Eating with my boys in German and Austrian beer halls, visiting the birthplace and home of Mozart, walking the streets he walked, touring and learning about the Hapsburg family that ruled Austria for 600 years. Over and over, I felt a delight from travel and exploration that was just as amazing and fun as it had been twenty years ago.

Some things in life don't stack up to our memories. There've been many times when I've convinced my boys to watch a movie from my childhood that, partway through, I realized had not held up. But this! This was just as amazing to me, and I was thrilled that it had the same effect on my boys.

One of the many quotes I've seen on social media that's been attributed to Socrates and Charlemagne is, "To have a second language is to possess a second soul." Whoever said this, I agree because it's how I felt when speaking another language.

The boys and I have similar passions, and one of those is history. When we were in Salzburg and Vienna, we visited castles and ancient gardens, and we saw huge collections of armor and the living quarters of royal families. We kept coming across Roman ruins. I didn't know much about Roman history at the time, but we learned that Vienna had once been on the northern edge of the Roman empire.

Standing in a square outside the Hofburg Palace in Vienna is where a big *Yes, and!* happened. There's a giant hole that you can peer down into and see the remains of a huge building from when Vienna was a Roman outpost on the northern border of the Empire. I stood on the edge of this hole, looking down at the brick and concrete remains of a building made by the Romans two thousand years ago. The hole was rather deep as it held maybe a two-story building whose roofline was at today's ground level. This was the third time we'd seen something like this on the trip.

I distinctly remember saying to my boys, "This is amazing. If this was the edge of the empire, imagine how incredible the capital must be! I think we should make plans to see the center of the empire that built this." In that moment, at the edge of this ruin, an idea was born that would carry us into some new adventures.

> *In that moment, at the edge of this ruin, an idea was born that would carry us into some new adventures.*

On the plane ride home, I did some serious reflecting. I was thrilled at how much fun we'd had, even though it rained the first full week of our travels. I looked at a picture of the boys in Iceland, standing in the rain on the edge of a dormant volcano. It was cold. We were jet lagged. Alex had a really bad cold, but both boys were grinning ear to ear! When we arrived in Salzburg, we'd walked a mile in the rain to get to the convent-turned-hostel where I'd made reservations. We were having fun on our adventure and no one complained, even when our cheap umbrellas turned inside out in the strong wind as we made our way through the cold, wet, rainy streets toward our shelter.

I thought about how much fun it had been to speak German again. We'd had richer experiences because we could connect with people in their own language. One afternoon when the boys were too exhausted to walk around anymore, I went for a stroll to visit some of the shops around the historic part of town. In a tiny shop that sold candles, I struck up a conversation in German with a local. She called the bag for my purchase a word that I wasn't familiar with. She let me know it was an Austrian dialect. We then proceeded to have a really fun conversation about dialect, and I was able to teach her words from the Swabian dialect I had learned twenty years earlier. It was so much fun!

Saying *please* and *thank you* in the native language can open many doors and hearts. People are proud of their heritage, culture, and history. When they meet a stranger who's taken the time to learn and appreciate their culture, a magical thing seems to happen. For us, after a little chit chat, they were soon telling us about some must-see places or offering tips and tricks we wouldn't have known. They did that because they knew we respected their culture. The hours and hours I'd spent as a kid learning and practicing were now connecting us with strangers and opening doors to adventure we wouldn't have seen otherwise.

As I reflected on all of this and the idea of going to Rome, a thought occurred to me. Maybe I could learn Italian! I'd wanted to do that for so many years, but the idea just sat there like a collector's toy wrapped in its box, never opened.

Yes and!

I played with this idea and remembered that when I was young, I often dreamed of working or living in Europe one day. But that idea had died as I added to my list of responsibilities as a young dad, homeowner, and worker.

Yes and!

I remembered my brother had told me that, because of the circumstances of my grandfather's immigration, we might be eligible for dual citizenship in Italy.

Yes and!

My buddy, Mike, who introduced me to improv, told me about a website he was using where he worked with language tutors all over the world via Skype.

Yes and!

My friend Ken told me about Duolingo, a language learning app where you can study on your own wherever you are.

Yes and!

By now, I had a new energy I hadn't felt in many, many years. It was just like the feeling I'd had as a kid when it was near an upcoming holiday or my birthday—that feeling of excitement and expectation. I was so excited to be diving into a whole field of things I was passionate about: language, history, art, and culture—and without really being conscious of it myself at the time.

> *By now, I had a new energy I hadn't felt in many, many years.*

My father had died the year before, and because of the circumstances of my parents' divorce, we hadn't known each other well. And yet, during the bits of time we had spent together, he'd always spoken fondly and longingly of Italy and Sicily. But he never went there. What he thought and felt about Italy was what he'd learned second-hand from his parents, who were immigrants. I wanted to experience Italy firsthand.

So, I dove in. I signed up for Italian lessons. At first, I couldn't construct a sentence. When I heard people speaking Italian, it sounded beautiful to me, but I couldn't understand a thing they said, just an incomprehensible but beautiful melody that conjured memories of my grandparents. By using Duolingo, tutors, flash-cards, and a bit of Rosetta Stone, I gradually began to learn.

At this same time, I dove into pursing dual citizenship with Italy, and I had to track down documents that spanned 112 years—my grandparents' birth, marriage, immigration, and death certificates along with similar documents for my parents, myself, and my children. It was a grand scavenger hunt through time and important milestones in my family's history. Official certificates for eight births, four deaths, three marriages, two divorces, and important immigration documents that traced my family from a little village in Sicily to the United States one hundred years ago! As someone who loves history, this was a complete joy.

In the course of my research, a cousin in Saint Louis suggested that I reach out to a Sanfilippo man in Sicily. I sent a friend request via Facebook and we communicated with Google Translate. I soon learned that not only was he my dad's cousin, but he lived in the very house my grandfather had been born in. He suggested that the boys and I come visit, so he could introduce us to our family.

Yes and!

My new cousin said that none of them spoke English, so I knew it was up to me to learn Italian. I doubled my efforts. Soon he suggested that we should talk with an app on my iPhone called WhatsApp. Yikes!! I still couldn't say much of anything in Italian, so I put off his first few requests. He persisted.

Finally, we spoke. The moment I heard his voice and accent I had chills. I heard the accent of my grandparents. They had died over twenty years ago, but those sounds echoed in my head. It wasn't an Italian accent, it was a distinct Sicilian accent, and I'd made a living connection with my grandparents. My cousin was amazingly patient with me as I looked up words and phrases on my phone and with a dictionary. I was slowly learning to communicate in the language of my family.

As I began looking through travel books for what to see, I realized how little I actually knew about Italy and its amazing history. So, I began listening to history books during my commutes and walks. I listened to audio books about the thousand-year history of Venice, the birth of the Renaissance in Florence, a biography of Michelangelo, Leonardo, and a book about the history of Sicily going back 4000 years, That sounds like a lot, but to me it was like candy. I couldn't—and can't—get enough.

Yes and!

Roughly five months later we landed in Italy and explored Venice, Florence, and Rome before hopping on a plane to Sicily, where we made our way to the very town where my grandparents were born. During our three days in Trappeto, my sons and I met forty cousins. The local newspaper even did an interview with us because I was the grandson of the brother who had left and never returned.

In addition to discovering a part of me that I thought I'd put away forever, the boys got a glimpse of my experience with my grandparents, whom they'd never known. When I was little and we visited my grandmother, she and her children mostly spoke Sicilian, and my brother and I would sit quietly and try grasp what was being said. They were now having that same experience.

It had only been a year since we stood at the edge of a Roman ruin looking down into history. I'd felt the tug in my heart toward something I couldn't fully explain then and am still working to understand. Since then, I've gone from a level 0 Italian speaker to working toward an intermediate level. If my goal had been to simply communicate at a basic level, I'd be finished. But I'm having so much fun that I want to keep going. I want to be able to dive into the wealth of Italian literature. To take courses in art history in Italian in Italy.

I've also read or listened to about fourteen books on Italian or Roman history for the simple pleasure of it. I now know so much about my family history and heritage, and I've secured my dual citizenship with Italy and the United States. All of this and so much more has unfolded from that single moment of awe when I said *Yes and!*

What about you? What dreams have you packed away? What keeps tugging at you? What would be fun that you haven't tried yet? Listen to that pull! Say yes! Read that book, ask your friend to hang out, make the plans. Take that class. Try it. You have no idea what will grow from that one small action, no idea what seeds will be planted. The people and circumstances you could attract could very well stun you. As Goethe said, "Whatever you can do, or dream you can, begin it. Boldness has genius, power and magic in it."

Chapter
FIVE

Follow the Fun

Many people die with their music still in them. Too often it is because they are always getting ready to live. Before they know it time runs out.

~ OLIVER WENDALL HOLMES

BEFORE I SAID YES, I said no—a lot. I said no to my ideas, dreams, thoughts, preferences, wants, and needs because I was afraid to say no to others: to my wife, to my work, to my family. Early in life, I'd developed a passion for language, art, history, culture, and travel, but I said no to all of them, all the time. Until I didn't.

It would be easy to blame others for my pattern of denying myself. Blame my ex-wife. Blame my mom. Blame all my obligations. Blame my profession. Blame my possessions. Blame society. Blaming would be so easy—but it would be wrong. I had done this to myself. I had buried the interests that were inside me. I was afraid to act on them. I justified not following them. I was afraid to do something that no one else was doing. It seemed wrong and selfish to pursue what I wanted, so I said no to myself, time and time again. As a kid being raised as a Catholic, I heard or read "But when I grew up, I put away childish things" and I completely absorbed that lesson.

I actually thought I'd successfully buried my desires by terming them "not practical," but they continued to tug at me, no matter how hard I tried to push them down. They were a shadow inside me. My heart longed for those forgotten things like you'd long for a lost love. What should have been a comma along my way to a full and satisfying life had become a period, as if my crowning achievements had already come and gone.

> *It seemed wrong and selfish to pursue what I wanted, so I said no to myself, time and time again.*

Let me give you an example. For years, I thought about how much I missed my college days. I loved college. It was a period of massive, intentional growth and freedom for me, picking my classes and having so much time to learn and study. I was thrilled to be there. I loved the giant library. It was a storehouse of amazing knowledge for me to explore. To learn from people who had their Ph.D. was difficult, challenging, and amazing. I loved browsing through the bookstore and buying ten or more new books, twice a year. I thrived on being with others who were also there to learn and grow.

I dreamed about going back to school, but I'd started my career as a financial planner and entrepreneur, and that didn't really warrant getting an MBA. I was paid for results, not titles or degrees. I had no manager to impress, just clients who depended on me to help them and to be there for them. With my family obligations and time constraints, I couldn't justify the time or expense to go back to school; that felt like a vanity project. But it was something I really wanted to do. Not getting my MBA, just going back to college. On the weekends while I was doing yard work, I'd often daydream about when my kids were grown and I had enough time and money to go back to college. College! Being back in a university was a dream that wouldn't die.

One evening as I was going through my healing process, I felt wonderful. I was building my dining room table, and I had an improv lesson that night. A feeling came upon me that was so strong that it stopped me in my tracks—kind of like when you smell something that takes you back to your grandma's kitchen or you hear a song that reminds you of your first crush. I realized I had the same feeling that I associated with being in college. I could feel it buzz through me like an electric current. I was learning and exploring art by making things and acting. I was gaining new skills, meeting new people. Growth! This was what I had wanted all those years. The feeling of *becoming*. The mental rush of growth was what I'd been craving; it had nothing to do with paying tuition or sitting in a classroom. It was one of the most exciting self-discoveries I've ever experienced.

> *The mental rush of growth was what I'd been craving; it had nothing to do with paying tuition or sitting in a classroom.*

My mind flashed back to all my years of education. I remembered that when I took history, art history, philosophy, English, and German, it felt natural. I'd thought that those were just easy classes that I got to take, but my business classes were the important classes. The business classes were the adult things. The humanities were the childish things—an understanding that had been reinforced by my upbringing and the example set by my mom. Through her passion and interest for so many things, she helped implant a curiosity in me, but those kinds of things were for free time, if at all. She was a single mom, working fifty-plus hours a week to pay the bills. She was also a child of the depression, a time when people did what they had to do and fun was a luxury.

When I put away my childish things, I picked up the pieces of life that promised the American Dream. Like a house in the suburbs that required so much time and money that I had no time for the childish things. Instead, I had to do adult things like cut the grass, clean the gutters, and fix the toilet, because that's what adults do. Everything and everyone in my world reinforced this. To make it worse, we had a charming century-old house that had lots of "fun" old house projects that had a way of consuming all our time and money. When I wasn't actually doing the labor myself, I was spending money to get it done. I was exchanging my life in terms of time and money—which I'd received for giving up other bits of my life and time—for things that I didn't want to do.

> *I was exchanging my life in terms of time and money—which I'd received for giving up other bits of my life and time—for things that I didn't want to do.*

In my dying moments, I won't give two thoughts about how nice my lawn looked. In the past eight years, I've never once thought, *I wish I was cutting the grass,* or edging the lawn or any number of chores I never liked doing in the first place. In my quest to give up childish things, rather than doing the things that brought me joy that I'd craved for more than two decades, I filled my life with things that were mind-numbing and meaningless to me. I can hear a chorus of voices—one of which used to be mine—saying,

"This is just a part of being an adult. That is life. You don't always get to do what you want." True, but we can construct our lives to minimize those things. Ah—I still get excited about this!!

This was an accidental discovery, a byproduct of my divorce and the fact that I missed my kids. Every other week, I didn't see my boys. Those first few months without them brought an empty ache that was quite painful. I got all kinds of advice from friends about "getting back out there." Go meet someone. Get on a dating app. Go to a bar. Do something. I tried all those things and they felt empty. But as I began saying yes to the things I wanted—what I was interested in, the childish things—I was, without knowing it, following the fun.

Follow the fun is another improv lesson that I've carried with me offstage. Within the context of improvisational theater, the idea is to begin a scene with a grounded character (meaning real, not crazy/zany) and an emotion from which you and your scene partner can build a base reality. In the course of exploring that relationship, because of the inherent absurdity of life, the two of you discover the fun or ridiculous thing and play with that. It's not about making jokes; it's about revealing the comedy of our existence. Follow the fun. That's all I was doing, wasn't it?

In trying to climb out of the darkness of my divorce and the death of my parents, I started to say yes to those desires I'd long held back. It wasn't like I'd found some new great strength to do this, but rather, it was because I was too beaten down to fight any longer. Too worn down to fight myself. Whether it was God, the universe, or some random synchronicity, these painful experiences opened doors that I'd been holding shut. I would never ask for the pain I went through, but it put several things into alignment that allowed me the space to make this discovery. For twenty years I'd used my willpower to delay this satisfaction. To keep saying no to myself. To be happy with a daydream about yesterday instead of taking action today. Once I grasped the idea that I could say yes to myself, I cherished it.

I had some friends who were excited about the new things I was doing but implied, in one way or another, that I was having a mid-life crisis or had developed some new coping methods because of my situation. That was not true. When I finished building my own table and bed, I knew this was how I wanted to live my life. I wanted to design and organize my life around growth and learning. Stepping stones. This led to an incredibly fun period of making art that I could use in my everyday life. I learned that I *needed* to have an artistic outlet.

How about you? What dreams have you set aside? What keeps pulling at you? Whispering to you?

Sometimes the things that bother, annoy, or attract us are shadows of ourselves that we recognize in others. For example, for many years when I was trapped in a life I didn't like, I had a negative reaction when someone talked about something they'd done years ago that had brought them great joy—like being great at some subject or sport, or to have been a Boy Scout, or to have played a musical instrument. At the same time, they were saying no to themselves about learning an exciting new skill that could further their career or help them start a whole new one. This really annoyed me. Without realizing it, I was actually seeing myself in those people. My frustration—and sometimes judgement—wasn't about them but about my own lack of action. My own self-sabotage.

Now I follow the fun. What brings me joy and happiness right now is my Italian. I'm quite conscious of the grammar and vocabulary I still need to learn, but I've grown from knowing nothing to an intermediate level in only two and a half years. I know

I'll make that much progress again in the next few years. After that, who knows what's next? As I continue to follow the fun, will I learn Sicilian? French? Spanish? Portuguese? Dutch? Who knows? I'll follow the fun and figure it out as I go.

What are you saying no to? Do you want to learn a language? Play an instrument? There are so many things we have to learn to be adults in life, but what are the passions that keep calling you? Follow them. You don't have to wait to descend into a dark period of life like I did. Give yourself permission to do these things now. With the internet and free libraries, we have nearly all of humanity's history and wisdom at our fingertips. Explore those things that are calling you. Open your eyes to the freedom you can create and say yes to the rest of your life.

Holding up the Mirror

*Looking outwards has got to be
turned into looking into oneself.
Discovering yourself provides you
with all you are, were meant to be,
and all you are living from and for.*

~ CARL JUNG

I THINK I WAS IN COLLEGE when I first read the directive *know thyself.* I remember thinking, "Cool. Good idea, but how?!" No adult had ever suggested that this was important. Nothing in my school or church experience gave me any indication that this was even a thing, much less offered instruction about how to do it.

Now that I think about it, most of my upbringing was about being told who I was. What I could and couldn't do, be, have, aspire to. What I needed to believe. How I needed to act and dress and behave. It's no wonder I didn't have my own back. Because of this, I doubted my instincts and buried my passions. I bought into what society expected; I hadn't been exposed to the tools and skills I needed to peel back my own layers. I didn't know how to shine light into the shadow of my being.

> **Now that I think about it, most of my upbringing was about being told who I was.**

When I graduated college and began my career, I read everything I could get my hands on about success. Like a good disciple and follower, I read from all the big self-help and success gurus; in fact, I credit a great deal of what I accomplished materially and financially to following their advice and instruction. The problem was that I didn't know *me,* and they were giving advice on how to obtain external things. More income, more things, more money. *How much money do you want to make? What kind of house do you want to live in? What kind of clothes do you want to wear? What are your goals for everything you want to do, have, and be?* How could I answer these questions when I didn't know who I was or what I wanted?

In a college psychology class and from further reading, I'd learned the term *self-actualization* and had read about enlightenment, but I didn't know what those things meant. I just thought they sounded cool. I'm certain I have old notebooks somewhere with "be enlightened" as a ten-year goal, along with "be successful," and "get in shape," the vague goals that twenty-something Carlo longed for. I ended up working really hard and fulfilling a definition of success called The American Dream, which was like trying to fill a black hole by scooping sand with a tiny plastic shovel.

It was an impossible dream. I was in a constant state of waiting. Striving but never arriving. Working, building, saving, delaying for "one day." One day I'll have enough. One day the house will be right. One day. One day. One day. I was working, studying, and learning how to have more but not how *to be.* Not how to understand. Gaining skills but not wisdom. Earning a living but not a life—all the clichés. It was an empty and futile quest, but I didn't know anything else and, even if I did, there wasn't time for anything else in my life. Further, I was in a career that was all about money. As a financial planner, I'd been trained to help other people with their money. How much money do you need for this, that, and more? How much was enough?

This is why I say that so many things I'm experiencing now didn't come from out of the blue. They didn't come because I was sad or hurt. My pain and suffering served to break down my resistance and willpower to fight. Death, not just of my parents but also my marriage—and all the roles, patterns, rituals, and relationships that go with that—was destructively painful but also transformative. Like a blooming prairie the season after a wildfire.

When I try to explain all the changes and growth I've experienced, it's difficult because the changes and growth weren't linear. It wasn't an A to B to C process. It was more like the 3-D fractal patterns that repeat themselves over and over again in nature—in trees, lightning, and blood vessels, etc. For me, these fractals—these repetitions—were the coaching and therapy that I received.

The most powerful thing I gained during that time was the ability to look at myself. And the first step was to seek professional help. My decision to step into a therapist's office was one of the most important of my life.

> *The most powerful thing I gained during that time was the ability to look at myself.*

Aside from their education, experience, and training, my therapists offered me an outside perspective from someone who wasn't my spouse, sibling, or friend. They didn't have any skin in the game. They had no history with me. They weren't going to see me during the holidays. They were simply there to help me, to show me things I couldn't or didn't want to see by gently and repeatedly holding up a mirror that reflected my actions, emotions, and ways of being.

That mirror showed me deeply painful things about myself. Even though my therapists had objectives, sometimes I could see a bit of pain or discomfort in their eyes as they delivered the tough love I needed—that I actually wanted and was willing to pay for.

I was broken down. I was done fighting, not by choice, but because I had nothing left to fight with. In less than five years, I'd lost my mom, my stepdad, my father, my marriage, my home, many friends, and so much more. I'd experienced divorce as a child but not as an adult. I lost friends who didn't know what to do with single Carlo living in the city, digging through warehouses of old lumber and building things. Who was that guy?!

Some couples didn't know what to do with their newly single friend. They tried to connect me with their other single friends, so I'd be a "normal" couple again. Just like them. If that didn't work, they'd invite me to fewer things because my singleness made them uncomfortable. At first it really hurt me to learn about an event to which I wasn't invited that I would have attended had I been married or in a relationship. But over time I was OK with it because I was on a new path. Alone but not lonely.

My pain and new status in life helped me to be open to seeing what my therapists showed me— but not always immediately. Like when my brother said that I wasn't myself in my marriage. Or when my first therapist said I couldn't write off a decade of my life. Or when Coach Elli told me to love myself.

My last therapist, Greg, really opened my eyes. He told me that the hurt that some people had caused me was actually my own shadows and scars that lived deep inside me that were now being reflected back to me. And the beautiful, loving things that I longed to receive from others were things that were already inside me that I refused to see, acknowledge, or set free.

But back to the beginning. At the end of my very first therapy session, my therapist said she thought that meeting with her would be helpful, and she agreed to take me as a client/patient. She asked if I had any questions.

The planner in me, in all seriousness, leaned in and asked "How will we know when we're done? What are we trying to accomplish?"

She smiled at me like the wise woman she was, one who had heard that question a million times. She said it was a typical question, particularly for people who worked in the financial field because we normally saw things as checklists to complete or objectives to be conquered. In fact, I wouldn't understand her reply for two or three more years.

"It's a process," she answered.

I nodded. Not in agreement, but to acknowledge that I was going to trust her. A process.

So, I began the process. I worked with this woman for about a year and then she retired. She referred me to another therapist who helped me as I went through my divorce. I then took a break while I dealt with my mom's death. Later I worked with Coach Elli and finally Greg.

Since learning and growing are passions of mine, it makes sense that I'd make myself the subject of my search. I was ready to look inward for insights and understanding, and I was ready to accept help. I began to understand my patterns, emotions, and ways of being that I'd carried for decades, and I decided to turn my energy inward. It was fun and energizing to study Italian or learn about the Renaissance, but what I actually needed to understand was *Carlo*. I knew deep in my core that if I didn't take this time to look honestly at myself, I'd keep repeating the patterns that had gotten me where I was. It was and is a process, and somewhere in the middle of it, I began to understand. Socrates gives the advice that "The unexamined life is not worth living." I was learning a very valuable skill.

Looking At Versus Looking As

In his book *The Untethered Soul: The Journey Beyond Yourself,* Michael Singer offers an example that will prove helpful here. He explained that when we go to a movie and sit in a dark room to watch, the synchronization of light and sound can pull us in so deeply that we may literally jump to get out of the way of a bad guy or car crash. We can become frightened or sad, or experience any other range of emotions; however, if something malfunctioned and the sound and lights weren't in synch, we'd be very aware that we were sitting in a dark room full of strangers with our feet resting on a sticky floor. And, he said, this form of entertainment uses only two of our five senses. Imagine how immersed we'd be if a movie incorporated smell, touch, and taste! We'd lose touch with reality, and that's exactly what happens when we look at ourselves through our current state of awareness. *What?* How else could we see the world??

That was my reaction when I began trying to wrap my mind around this concept. So, I dove in deeper. Each author, each book I read, was like a stepping-stone that led me to the next. The combination of putting my defenses down, being open to change, and working with professionals who gently and persistently held up that mirror showed me my own patterns. It allowed me to see where I was holding myself back. Where I was afraid to trust myself. Afraid to speak my truth. This part of the process gave me the strength to say yes to the things I'd buried for so long. To emerge from a darkness. To wake up. It wasn't a *single thing* that created change but a *big system* that created change. Saying yes and the stepping-stones. A complicated and beautiful fractal.

When I'd honed the skill of looking at my behaviors, patterns, thoughts, and motives—and said yes to the things that pulled me—I felt like I'd developed an allergy to anything that didn't align with that energy. As my new way of being emerged, more and more pieces of my old life didn't quite work for me anymore.

> *As my new way of being emerged, more and more pieces of my old life didn't quite work for me anymore.*

As a society, we don't give people the tools they need to gain self-awareness. If anything, there's a stigma against it. Between the rugged individualism that defines success and negative associations with therapy and mental health, many people—including my younger self—have an aversion to getting help, looking inward, and doing the hard work. We spend years in school and years mastering our professions. Countless hours go into gaining knowledge of the things that interest us, but no part of our education helps us gain self-knowledge.

Investing time, money, and lots of energy into getting to know myself has helped me grow in ways I'm still discovering. And that's what is most exciting to me. I'm not done, and I won't be until I check out of this life.

We can't be afraid of not being done, or maybe we shouldn't. I once had a conversation with a very successful entrepreneur about this very thing. He told me his motto was, "If you're green, you're growing. If you're ripe, you're rotten." He went on to tell me that he constantly pushes himself to learn new things. His pearl of wisdom was new to me, and I remind myself of this often.

Gaining self-knowledge and awareness has not only affected my personal life, but also my professional life—and a big piece of that is my business. During my extreme life changes, I attended a workshop with a branding expert. He led the group to do an exercise where we thought back through our childhoods and tried to make connections between the events in our early years and our professions. I made the connection quickly, and it hit me hard.

My early childhood and our lack of resources had driven me to my profession. That shadow of fear drove me to study finance and to enter the field of personal financial planning. I wanted to understand money and conquer it. Eighteen-year-old Carlo didn't know that but, in that workshop, I made the connection. I wanted to help others so they wouldn't be consumed by that fear.

At the same time, I began resenting my company. I didn't want to do things the way I'd always done them. Simply helping people to get a good rate of return on their investments compared to a benchmark felt empty. It was empty. So, I transformed my business in a way that aligned with who I now was—the person I'd always been but had buried. I know I've helped my clients in ways that I couldn't have before. I have deeper, better, more genuine relationships with them because I'm showing up as myself. We have deeper conversations, and the same is true for my team.

The exciting thing is that it's not done! It is a process, and I plan on living a life of growth and discovery to the end.

Knowing thyself is a process. We have depths and layers akin to an ocean. If you think you're done learning something, chances are you're swimming on the surface, unconscious of the shadowy depths below you that can reveal a richer and more meaningful life—if you have the courage to dive into your own depths! If you want to grow, you must be prepared to look at the ugly things. Look at them and understand where they come from. How they are driving you? How can you learn and grow from them?

A deeper, richer world awaits you if you continually shine light into the recesses of your being, whether you're the one holding the mirror or someone else is holding it for you.

Getting Pulled into a Bigger World

The purpose of life, after all, is to live it,
to taste experience to the utmost,
to reach out eagerly and without fear
for newer and richer experience.

~ ELEANOR ROOSEVELT

BACK TO MY ITALIAN JOURNEY. This experience has included so much synchronicity and serendipity that I'm no longer surprised by anything that happens in life. I'm simply along for the ride. It's not like I'm getting pulled downstream and am hanging onto a life preserver—no—it's more like surfing. I'm being pushed forward by something powerful, and I'm riding on top of it. I don't control the wave, but my decisions and actions make micro changes to the direction it takes me. After decades of thrashing against the current, this is so much more fun!

At some point in my therapy—post-furniture making and just a few years into my improv journey—I was making a lot of progress in my life, learning new things, and meeting new people. I had an overwhelming feeling that I was being pulled *toward* something. I'd established a regular meditation practice and was consciously trying to expand my awareness, experiencing things I wouldn't have understood before. One of those was the feeling of utter expansion. I remember talking to Greg, my therapist, about this a number of times. I couldn't quite put the feeling into words, but it was powerful, and it was real. I had the sensation that I was expanding beyond what was happening in my life at that moment.

> *I had an overwhelming feeling that*
> *I was being pulled* toward *something*

A year or so later when I was on my way home from Germany and Austria with my boys, I felt like a seed had been planted to take a journey to Italy. Fast-forward one year, and I was in Italy having dinner in the village of my grandparents. Staring at the same sea they experienced every day as children—with my own children!

Before I went on that trip, I'd crammed for five months to learn enough Italian to get by. Now I was determined to continue that learning. I wanted to go beyond simply ordering a meal and asking for the bill. I wanted to have conversations. I wanted to be able to read books and watch movies. Tell jokes and understand the puns and irony.

The audiobooks for learning Italian got me off the ground. I picked up tons of vocabulary and basic sentence structure for present tense, but I needed more than that. I worked via Skype with Valentina, my friend and Italian tutor in Rome, but I also explored some classroom options at a university near me.

I looked online and saw the course descriptions and requirements to earn a degree in Italian, and I got really excited. Then

I found the page with the tuition prices. A single three-hour class cost $3,000, plus books, miscellaneous fees, and other ridiculousness. $3,000?! Ridiculous! My first thought was, *I could go over there for less than that!* I had just planned and executed a three-week vacation with my two sons for about $6,000.

My second thought . . . *Why don't I?!*

I immediately searched for immersive language classes. I first looked in Florence because my boys and I had only spent a few days there, and there was so much more I wanted to explore. Symbolically, there couldn't have been a better place. Florence is known as the birthplace of the Italian Renaissance—home of Leonardo, Michelangelo, and the Medici family who supported so many of these artists. It's full of museums and lovely things to see. Florence is extremely walkable, and it's easy to get there by train from Rome. With my beginner-level Italian skills, it would also be like going into the shallow end of the pool. There are so many tourists in Florence that English is frequently spoken, so I wouldn't be totally dependent on my Italian—though by the end of the trip I found myself walking far away from the tourist areas to find restaurants where only Italian was spoken.

Two weeks of classes cost about $350. I found an Airbnb that was five minutes away from the school for only $75 per night, an entire apartment in a large building referred to as a palazzo. This was likely the former home of a wealthy family because it had a small courtyard with a cistern underneath. I knew from my studies that having a cistern would have been a great luxury centuries ago. Having a private water supply during a time of plague or invasion obviously had its benefits.

So, I went. I had my own apartment versus being in a dorm or a hotel. I had my own kitchen to cook in, to make coffee in while I studied and read. I could even do laundry! My airline ticket was free because of the points I'd accumulated on my credit card.

I wouldn't need a car, and my food costs traveled with me since I had to eat somewhere. I learned that one can eat far, far better in Italy than in America for the same budget. So, for around $1,500 I would get forty hours of classroom time with no more than eight students per class, multiple extra field trips around the city. Plus, when I wasn't in class . . . I was in Italy and could practice speaking the language every day.

YES AND, and YES PLEASE!

I signed up for a class, and the first week focused on Italian language and culture. I not only learned tons of grammar and vocabulary, but I also learned important things like how one should never order a *caffè latte* or cappuccino after lunch. The Italians decided centuries ago the right and wrong way to eat, drink, and cook things, and no cappuccino or *caffè latte* after lunch is a *molto importante* rule to follow. My Florentine teacher told me that there was a café that charged two euros for cappuccino at breakfast and one million euros after lunch! And the proprietor was serious about that.

During my second week, I studied art and architecture. We still focused on grammar and vocabulary, but the lessons were framed around art history and the architecture around Florence. The maximum class size was eight, but the first week there were only two of us. The second week it was just me and the teacher—private lessons! After a couple hours of classroom lessons, we went into the city to see the things we'd just studied. On the first Monday, the teacher asked me what I'd done over the weekend. I told her about my day trips to Bologna to see the oldest university in Europe and to Pisa to see the lovely church and famous tower. My trip to Pisa had been perfect because her worksheets for the day had named the church and tower of Pisa as examples of Romanesque architecture. We discussed the characteristics of this style and how it was unique from other later styles.

Then we went through the lovely Florentine streets to see more examples. My teacher would stop and ask, "What style is this? Where do you see an example of Romanesque columns?" Plus, she'd point out a million other interesting things.

"Ah! Do you hear that? That group is from Milan. Those people are from Naples." The accents and dialects are super-specific in Italy, and I was just dipping my toe into that new world.

For dinner, I frequently went to a place called Il Mercato Centrale, which means (as you can probably guess) the central market. The first floor was a giant market where vendors sold all kinds of amazing food. Produce, fish, meat, everything. The second floor, which looked like some kind of Victorian-era factory with lovely intricate ironwork, was a giant food court. But in this food court they served only amazing Italian food. I could get anything and everything, and I'd eat it at big tables around a giant bar in the center of the room. With the open seating arrangement, it was a great place to engage with people from all over.

I met so many amazing people during that time. One night, I shared my meal with a family from Rome. The man was my age and was working in Florence, accompanied by his wife and son. The grandmother was visiting from Rome. They invited me into their conversation and shared some unique food they'd ordered—a Roman specialty they felt lucky to find in Florence. Over and over again, the Italian people treated me like a prodigal son who'd returned home. Whenever they learned that I was the grandson of an immigrant who was exploring my heritage and the language of my family, they'd pull me in closer as if to welcome me home.

"Did you know this or that? Have you been here or there? Have you tasted this or that? You must! Come, come, let us show you!" Even now, it brings tears to my eyes to remember what a joy this journey has been.

Yes, I'd signed up for those two weeks of classes, but more importantly, I'd gotten an immersion experience, which took my language skills to another level and lit up my brain and soul like nothing else during my years of study. And here I was—in Florence.

> *I'd gotten an immersion experience, which took my language skills to another level and lit up my brain and soul like nothing else during my years of study.*

Florence, like most medieval and Renaissance cities, is small and walkable. It had to be because people . . . well, they walked. After class each day, I walked and walked and walked. According to the app on my phone, I walked nearly two hundred miles during those two weeks. Most days, I wasn't actually going anywhere. It was just about the walk. I wanted to explore the streets where Michelangelo grew up. Where Leonardo DaVinci lived. To sit in places and see versions of what they'd seen.

I even got a two-week pass for a local gym, and I worked out to keep up my routine. On the way to the gym, I passed by the Cathedral of Santa Maria del Fiore. If you've ever seen a picture of Florence, you've likely seen this cathedral. Dazzling white and green marble topped with a reddish tile roof. Lovely! The dome of the Cathedral is hugely important in terms of the Renaissance. The fall of Rome pulled humanity backward in so many ways. So many technologies and discoveries were lost. One of those was how to build a dome. Before this structure, a domed building had not been constructed in Europe for nearly six centuries.

Though the technology and know-how to build a giant dome no longer existed, the Florentines began construction of the cathedral in 1296 with plans for a giant octagonal base that would eventually be its foundation. They were so confident that they'd eventually figure it out that they proceeded with the construction. Can you imagine that kind of confidence?

And they did figure it out. In 1420, Filippo Brunelleschi, after winning a competition for designs, began constructing the dome and completed it sixteen years later. A dome hadn't been built for six hundred years, so how did he do it? Brunelleschi went to Rome and studied many of the surviving monuments and buildings, particularly the Pantheon. The Pantheon was a temple that had been built over 1,500 years before this cathedral project. Built during the time of Augustus Caesar at the dawn of the first millennium, the Pantheon had a dome that survived the fall of the Roman empire and was in use. Brunelleschi climbed up in the structure to study it, and he eventually reverse-engineered it. He went back to Florence and built the dome—without using any scaffolding.

This is what I got to walk by every day. Aside from being an architectural wonder that caused an explosion of new discoveries and construction, including the dome of St. Peters that Michelangelo designed, it is beautiful, clad in white and green marble with a red tile roof. I could stare at it for hours. In fact, I have.

In Florence, the birthplace of humanity's Renaissance, I realized I was in the middle of *my own personal renaissance*. A city that helped usher in a time of the rebirth of so much lost knowledge. The birth of humanism. The birth of a movement that would usher in the Enlightenment. All at a time when I was going through the most transformational and enlightening time of my life. I soaked in every bit of it I could—for half the cost of a university class. By listening to my instincts, following the fun, and "yes and-ing," here I was.

I savored and enjoyed this time as much as I could. I even experienced a snowfall in Florence. It hadn't snowed there in over a decade, and when about an inch of snow fell over the city, it practically shut down. Schools and stores were closed. I saw tiny one- to two-foot tall snowmen around the city. Italian snowmen! They call a snowman a *pupazzo di neve*. Literally, "a puppet of snow."

I enjoyed this rare treat with the citizens. Some would say that it was cold, and we were having "bad weather," but I was thrilled to be there. Plus, I got to wander the streets with the locals instead of mobs of tourists brandishing selfie sticks. It was lovely.

Too soon, I was home again. My tutor, Valentina, was surprised by how much I'd learned, and she adjusted our lessons accordingly. I bumped our lessons to two hours per week and tried hard to study more when I could. I felt so happy doing this. I'd dreamed of being back in college for so long, and I'd accidently discovered that what I had actually longed for was learning and growth. I'd discovered another way to get that experience. I was doing it. I was learning and growing. It was like I could feel the new neural connections in my brain. My mind, heart, and soul were all lit up, and I was gaining more and more proficiency in my new language.

What else was possible? Where else could I go? I was determined to make my first trip a stepping-stone, not a capstone. Valentina suggested I visit Apulia—the part of Italy that looks like a heel. Specifically, she thought I should go to a city called Lecce, known as the "Florence of the South" because of its beautiful architecture. I reasoned that if I'd been taking classes at a normal pace, I'd spend $6,000 to $9,000 per year in tuition, assuming I took one class each semester and one or two during the summer. But I'd just received more hours of education in language, art, architecture, and the culture of my family for only $1,500! So, I started researching classes in Lecce, which were similar in price—although food and lodging were even less expensive than in Florence. I found an Airbnb for $40 per night that included breakfast. Sold!

I was on my way again in October. A couple of trains and planes later, the hosts for the Airbnb, Emilio and Isabella, checked me in. They were adorable and so kind and were very curious about why I'd come to their town. I explained how I'd reconnected with my family in Sicily, how I'd been studying Italian, and how my teacher and her fiancé in Rome were from Apulia. Emilio was quick to teach me about the relationship between southern Italy and Sicily. He told me that the name of the town my grandparents were from, Trapetto, was an old word that means *frantoio* in modern Italian or "mill."

After a bit of chit-chat, they showed me around the apartment where I'd be living for the next two weeks. They took me into the kitchen where there was an amazing spread of local food items on the table. Tiny fat cucumbers only grown in that part of Italy, fresh tomatoes, all kinds of local fruit. There were donut-shaped bread things that were hard as a rock, but after you soaked them in water for ten seconds, they softened up and were quite good with tomatoes, olive oil, and other yummy things to choose from. Emilio said he'd collected the honey from his bees, and he'd made his own olive oil, which had won an award for the best olive oil in Apuglia the year before. I was blown away.

We chatted a bit about the process of making olive oil, and Emilio mentioned that he was going to start harvesting olives the following week. He asked if I would like to join him. Without hesitation I said, "Yes!" I'd always been curious about this ancient activity, which the Greeks had been doing since 3500 BC. Isabella said she'd put a meal together and we could make an afternoon out of it. I was in heaven, and I'd only just arrived. It was amazing that they were as thrilled to share this experience with me as I was to participate in it.

The next week I got a message that asked me if I could join them on Thursday.

YES!!

Right after my class, Isabella picked me up. We drove about an hour straight south to the very end of Italy's heel. We wound around some tiny roads and up the hills overlooking the sea into orchards of olive trees until we found Emilio.

He took me around the property and showed me examples of the three types of olive trees.

"This one is native to Italy. These over here were brought by the Greeks when they arrived thousands of years ago. That variety was brought here by Arabs who controlled this part of the peninsula for a time after the fall of Rome."

After a quick lesson about the olives we'd be harvesting, we went back to the house and sat at a giant outdoor table. Isabella had brought a spread of food including an ancient dish that the Greeks believed Hercules ate for strength, a spicy bread called *pizzo*, olive oil Emilio had just made yesterday, homemade wine, and for dessert, a homemade liqueur called *Padre Peppe*. It was a liquor made from walnuts. All of this with a background of acres of olive trees and a view of the Ionian and Adriatic Seas.

After dinner, we strolled into the grove and found a tree with a giant green net under it. Emilio handed me a long pole that had a rake device on one end and a hose coming from the other. He fired up a compressor, turned a lever on the pole, and the rake started to move back and forth rapidly. He took the pole from me, raised it up to the branches full of olives, as the moving rake touched a branch, olives rained down on us like black and green hail. He set me loose for my own harvesting and thousands of olives fell down into the nets and occasionally bounced off my head. Periodically, we'd grab opposite sides of the net to gather the olives in the center, and then we worked together to dump them into crates and then onto a tiny truck. We only had a couple hours before the sun went down. It was tiring work, but I was in heaven. I could have stayed there for a week just working on the olive harvest and would have loved to see it all the way through to the pressing and bottling of the oil. I will absolutely do this one day soon.

This physical—and spiritual—experience was unreal and amazing, and I'll be forever grateful for it. Grateful for the pain that woke me up. Grateful for saying yes to getting help. Grateful for the strength to look inside myself and make changes. Grateful for the people who loved me and supported me when I was in pain. Grateful that I learned to say yes. Grateful that the university cost so much that, out of defiance, I looked for another solution.

> *This physical—and spiritual—experience was unreal and amazing, and I'll be forever grateful for it.*

This is why I felt that sensation of surfing. Being pushed along by some great force, and at the same time, working to stay on top of it. To balance and not fall, to keep going forward, although not in a straight line. Nothing could stop me now.

Peeling Off the Layers

The message that underlies healing is simple yet radical: We are already whole … Underneath our fears and worries, unaffected by the many layers of our conditioning and actions, is a peaceful core. The work of healing is peeling away the barriers of fear that keep us unaware of our true nature of love, peace, and rich interconnection with the web of life. Healing is the rediscovery of who we are and who we have always been.

~ BILL VAUGHAN

ALL THE GROWTH I EXPERIENCED felt more like a multi-leveled branching fractal than a linear checklist. So many things were happening at once, and I was expanding, growing, and forking in new directions, at different angles, and at a different pace than ever before. It was organic, non-linear, unpredictable—and natural. It started when my sister-in-law encouraged me to find my style, which led me to build my own furniture. At the same time, other things were happening that, from where I sit now, seem like obvious choices, but at the time they were scary—but also liberating.

My home was beginning to take shape in terms of furniture, and I knew I needed some art. Or rather, I wanted art. I'd never had the freedom to choose what I wanted to hang on the walls as an adult. When I divorced, the only things I took with me were my tools, clothes, books, some pictures, and an antique armoire. I distinctly remember walking through our house one last time. I looked at the art and decorations, and I felt like they weren't mine. I didn't really like any of it. I felt like I was leaving a hotel. When you check out of a hotel, you take your suitcase and leave the rest because it's not yours. That's what this felt like. Now I was in a new space for me and my boys, and it had lots of big blank walls that called for art—but what art?

At lunch one day, I was walking through a second-hand store that took very nice, donated items, sold them, and gave the profits to charity. As I meandered through, I came across a print of Picasso's *Don Quixote* propped against a couch. I hadn't read the whole story of Don Quixote at that point, but I knew enough of it. It's the story of a man who dreamt, read, and studied for years and years about the lives of knights. About adventure. About helping people (at least in his fantasy version of what being a knight was all about). About leaving home and seeing the world. About being and doing something important. Finally, Don Quixote donned the ancient armor of his ancestors and rode out into the world to face the dragons. He wanted to stop reading about the accomplishments and greatness of others and get a taste of it himself. To start living on purpose even if others didn't understand.

That was exactly how I felt. I had dreamt for so long about what it might be like to live my own truth. If I could go back to school, if I could have adventures, if I could be creative, if I could have fun. And, like the people in Don Quixote's life, I'm certain some people I knew thought me a bit mad. I wasn't attacking windmills, but I was doing all kinds of new things, and that made some people who knew me uncomfortable. Not because it was crazy, but because I wasn't following the script that they had in mind for me. This wasn't the box I was supposed to live in.

When I spotted the Picasso, I stopped in my tracks. I looked at the print in its thin metal frame and took note of the five-dollar price tag. I said, *Yes. This is going in my home. Because it's meaningful to me. It tells me a story. It validates my choice to live my truth, not what's expected. Not because it's what everyone else is doing. Not because of anything except it's what I feel pulled toward.*

After the purchase I drove straight to the hardware store because I didn't have any picture hangers. Then I headed home to find the place to hang it. I'll never forget how happy I felt. Walking around from room to room. All those empty walls were calling to me. *Here? Nah. There? Nope. Ah! I know. There's a short wall right by my front door. A wall I walk past every time I'm coming or going.* I held it up. *Yes! That's it.*

I'd found the place where I wanted to hang this art. A place that I'd see every day. A place where it would remind me to keep going. To be brave. To fight the dragons that were trying to pull me back to my old ways of not living or speaking my truth.

You see, at that moment my new life didn't feel totally real yet. It felt like I was just dabbling. But this picture felt right to me, and I wanted the strength to carry on like Don Quixote. Discovering this for myself felt so good.

It felt amazing to realize that I could create my world not just to be aesthetically pleasing, but to inspire me. In that moment,

I decided that I wanted the art in my home to tell me stories. To remind me of the things and ideals I aspire to do, have, and be. To remind me to be strong. To not quit. To keep going. Even if I felt alone.

> *It felt amazing to realize that I could create my world not just to be aesthetically pleasing, but to inspire me.*

I hung that picture next to my front door nine years ago, and it's still there.

At the same time, I was doing my work in therapy, working with my coach, and journaling. I was branching out and exploring myself artistically through building things and learning improv. Each step was a stepping-stone. Over the next several years, I slowly found more and more things to bring into my new condo. My boys found also found some things, and this space slowly turned into our home.

Without realizing it, I was building new muscles in this part of my life as I learned to listen to and trust myself more and more. The things that no longer fit me felt out of place, uncomfortable. In fact, my wardrobe was the next thing that changed.

I realized that I didn't really like my clothes. Maybe it's more accurate to say that I started to not like them. I'd never thought much about what I wore—I just wore what I thought I was supposed to wear. My first boss after college told me not to "dress like a dock worker" as I entered the financial services field. For the record, I have no issue with how dock workers dress. If that's how I looked, so be it. But others had an issue with it, so I began building a costume of how I was supposed to dress for my industry. At least that's what it felt like, especially when wearing a wool suit in Saint Louis in July when it was a million degrees with a billion percent humidity, plus or minus. Over the years, I did my best with wearing suits, but it always felt like I was wearing a costume. Like the decorations in my old home. They were nice, pleasant, fine—but not me. I was always thrilled to get home and take off my suit.

As I learned more about what I wanted, I began searching for things that felt more like me. I tried buying different versions of the same kinds of clothing but still wasn't happy. One day I was having a conversation with a buddy and he suggested I get help. He suggested that I work with a stylist and told me he'd heard good things about a company called The Trunk Club. I'd had several good experiences with getting expert advice by now, so I was open to this approach. I went online and filled out a brief form about myself, my clothing sizes, and what I was generally looking for. I was soon contacted by Ali from New York. She and I had a more detailed conversation, she explained how the program worked, and off we went! Soon I was getting "trunks" delivered to my office. A trunk was a cube-shaped box with eight to twelve items of clothing, personally selected for me. I hate shopping. Malls, in particular, overwhelm me. So, this was perfect.

> *As I learned more about what I wanted, I began searching for things that felt more like me.*

I had about a week to try things on and I could keep all of it, none of it, or anything in between. The best part was that, like the other professionals I worked with, Ali wasn't emotionally attached to the items she'd sent. Certainly, she and the company made money when I kept the items, but I could feel that they were trying to help me find things I liked. When I didn't like something, it provided feedback to help improve future trunks.

Eventually Ali had a good idea of what I wanted, and she suggested I try adding a few custom-made items to my mix. I knew this would be more expensive, but I was game. Not because I wanted to spend more money to show off; I was just determined to find my style. Something that felt like me. I was OK with splurging a bit, especially after I'd saved thousands of dollars by building my own furniture.

One day some Trunk employees showed up at my office, measured me, showed me a bunch of material samples, buttons, and combinations. A month or so later, I got a new jacket, vest, some pants, and shirts. I'd never worn anything that fit so well, and the combinations were unique. I finally felt happy to put those clothes on to go to work or to go out at night. I wasn't creating some radically new fashion trend, but I was starting to build a small inventory of things that fit me well and made me feel good. They were unique and stood out in a subtle way.

Especially wearing a vest. I've always liked vests, but I'd never had one that fit well. I really don't like wearing a suit and tie, but I want to look professional. Plus, I get hot easily and wearing clothing designed for eighteenth century London doesn't make sense in Saint Louis most of the time. Further, because not many people wear vests, my new clothes were perceived as more dressed up than when I wore a suit and tie. It was fun.

I changed my wardrobe because it was a small thing that I wanted. And an odd thing happened. People began to notice. Clients who, in fifteen years or more, had never said a thing about my clothes suddenly said things like, "Hey, that's a nice jacket. I like that vest! That shirt looks great."

I simply wanted to wear things that felt like me, and in the process of becoming more "Carlo," people took notice. It was validating. It gave me the same feeling as when people were excited about seeing my table or other furniture. Because I did something that felt right to me, that was in alignment with my instincts, people noticed things they'd never commented on before.

I've actually found some of my favorite clothes while traveling. Keep your eyes open. The more you're aware of who you are, the more easily you'll find what works for you. And like any kind of exercise, it's a muscle you have to build by using it.

"What's the deal with the beard?"

That was another change—my hair. Just like my clothing, for years I'd been cutting my hair the way I thought I needed to, so I could fit in with my industry. It was something I was very conscious about as I finished college. During my senior year, I let my hair grow out long enough to have a small ponytail and I grew a beard. I did it because I could, and I was certain that I wouldn't be able to for the next thirty years or so. If, one day, I lived long enough to retire, and I still had hair and the desire, then I could have facial hair and wear my hair any way I want—one day. I wore a ponytail for about a year until it was time to get a job and take things seriously. It was another example of "putting away childish things," and ultimately burying myself bit by bit to fit in.

That was in the early 1990s when casual office attire was still a few years away and facial hair was taboo. Twenty years later, I still carried that belief. But now—was it still true? Inertia held me in place until November 2016.

After that Presidential election, I was shocked by the result. Out of frustration, I didn't shave for a month. It was near the holidays, so I wasn't seeing many clients during that time. One day in December I looked in the mirror and a part of me said, *You need to shave.* Another part said, *Why? Why, do I have to? For the past five years you've been following your gut and learning to trust yourself. It's felt good, felt right, and you've gotten positive feedback from friends, family and clients. So why not embrace this too?*

I was in a new phase of life. A new stage of growth and development. Why couldn't I have a beard? Then fear set in and said, *What if some people don't like it? What if you're rejected? What if a client fires you?* Then, I thought, *That's OK. I'm forty-four years old. I provide an amazing service for my clients. I work hard for these families. I give up my time and sacrifice doing every other thing in the world I could be doing to help them—why can't I have a beard?*

So, I didn't shave. I had also just changed hair stylists. Micah had been cutting my hair for a few months now.

I went to see him after not shaving for several weeks and he said, "What's going on with your facial hair?

I said, "I think I'm going to grow a beard."

"$%#@ yeah you are!" he said.

And so, I did.

Oh man, the reactions were priceless. People weren't sure what to say, but they were sure to say something.

"What's . . . this?"

"Is this for hockey?"

"Are you going hunting"

"What's the deal with the beard?"

"What the hell have you done?!"

People asked questions, but I didn't lose any friends or clients, though many were interested and very curious.

Finally, I was able to articulate my motive for growing a beard. I'd been working really hard on myself for several years. I'd worked hard to live the life I wanted as I wanted. I saw that as a big part of my mission as an advisor. How could I say that I was an expert in helping people live their dreams if I wasn't living mine? My dream wasn't to dress up and be someone else. I wanted self-realization. Self-actualization. A new jacket, a piece of art, a piece of furniture, a beard, or a haircut don't provide any of those things, but being true to myself certainly felt like a step in the right direction. None of these things were permanent. None of them are who I am. They're things that felt good to me in that moment. At that time. Isn't that all we have? I fervently want to help my clients live the life they want. Even more important, I want my kids to live their lives. I want them to feel free to cut their own path.

It's been several years since I grew my beard, and I still get questions about it. But now I see it as a positive. I'm showing up as myself. I work hard to provide a service that's unique and different. For years I had to work really hard when I met people to get my point across. Part of that was because I showed up and looked like everyone else in my business. Same clothes, haircut, glasses, and same lingo. But, like everyone else, I'm different.

Who knows what I'll discover next? I'm just following the fun, and I hope you will too. I'm not married to anything I've done, and I'm not afraid to make more changes as life goes on.

Listen to what's pulling you and say yes. If you're afraid, start small and give it a try. It really is like building a new muscle. Each new thing will lead you to new discoveries, adventures, decisions, relationships, and opportunities that you can't see now. Keep listening to whatever whispers to you. Say yes. Take baby steps if you need to but keep moving in the direction of your dreams.

It's not the beard, the clothes, or my haircut, that's had a profound effect on my personal and professional life. It's me feeling confident enough to show up and be present as myself. I now have deeper connections with people because I'm showing up more and more whole. More and more Carlo.

Chapter
NINE

Retooling My Profession

This above all: to thine own self be true,
And it must follow, as the night the day,
Thou canst not then be false to any man.
~ SHAKESPEARE, *HAMLET*

I'D REACHED A CROSSROADS. By now, anything that didn't align with my inner being felt like a sharp pebble in my shoe. I had to get it out. It felt like a lie to live apart from my truth. Sometimes what bothered me was obvious and easy to change. Other times it took more work to figure it out.

The next big thing that had to change was my financial planning practice. But how could I change that? I had a business partner, employees, and all of our clients to consider. Just thinking about shaking things up felt like getting a divorce—and I didn't want that again.

There's an interesting backstory about how I got into this field. When I was five years old, my parents got divorced. All of a sudden, money became an issue. My mom, who'd been earning money by babysitting a few kids my age, immediately had to go back to work. We were never rich before, and now every penny counted. We always had food, clothes, and a home, but my mom worked tirelessly to make that happen.

She got a job as a secretary at McDonnell Douglas Corporation in the late 1970s and worked there until the early 1990s. In the early years, that meant she answered the phone for forty to fifty men. She typed all kinds of letters, memos, and— what sounds to me as supremely stressful—government contracts on which there could be no corrections. No whiteout. No mistakes. They had to be perfect. If she made one mistake on the last word of a page, she'd have to start over. Her work had to be perfect in that smoke-filled, noisy environment that played havoc with her allergies. She answered the phone and took messages for all those men, which sometimes included angry wives, kids, girlfriends, or other non-work-related calls because no one had a cell phone; there was no texting or emails or any other form of communication other than writing letters.

When the weekends rolled around, she sometimes worked on Saturdays to get the overtime pay. When she got home, she'd take the Saturday paper and comb through it, hunting for coupons. She compiled coupons and cross-checked recipes. Then went to several grocery stores to get the best deals for the giant meals she'd make us for the week.

This, I discovered later, was the birth of one of my shadows, something I call a Money Shadow™. In my case, it planted a great fear of lack in me. A great need to figure out money. How to earn enough. How much is enough? What if I run out? Before I entered high school, I started working to make money. I cut grass, I babysat, and I did all kinds of odd jobs to earn and save money. My mom made sure we had a savings account, and I added to it as often as I could.

This fear of lack had a profound impact on me and my future. In college, I was interested in so many subjects. Part of me wanted to dive into science. I had a huge passion for biology and nearly all the humanities were like candy to me. I could have easily taken a deep dive into art history, archeology, or a number of other areas. But fear drove me into finance. I had to be practical. I had to understand this thing that dominated and permeated so much of my childhood.

I originally studied German and Finance in hopes of doing some kind of international business. That's why, in 1993, I participated in an internship at a bank in Germany. During that month-long experience, I spent a week or so in the investment department. I sat silently in the advisor's office, who was quite kind and explained a great deal to me. When his clients came in, he explained that I was an American intern and asked their permission for me to sit quietly to observe and learn. Not one person refused.

One gentleman was quite happy to meet me. After peppering me with questions, he invited me to have dinner with his wife and him. I rode my bicycle to their beautiful home, and he told me about being released from a Russian POW camp during World War II. After Germany was conquered, it was divided in half by the Soviet Union. The other half, initially, was divided among Britain, France, and the United States before it was merged into West Germany.

When this client came home from the war, the area where he lived was on the border of the American and British sectors. He was sad to find that his wife, who had been his girlfriend back then, was in the British sector and that he was in the American sector. The American servicemen would sometimes take him to the British side so he could visit her. He told me all about how the

Marshall plan had impacted their lives and how grateful he was for the post-war efforts the Americans made. I realized that, in that quiet moment in their home, he was expressing his thanks to our entire country through me. I was humbled and honored and will carry that memory with me forever.

When I finished my internship and came back to America, I was curious about how I could use what I'd learned to help others. I soon had an opportunity to work at a financial planning company. I dove into it. Did what I was told to do. Watched the top performers. Asked them questions and took their advice.

In 1993, I was answering phones and typing labels. By 1996, I was licensed, was getting my own clients, and had gained the confidence that I could actually do this. In 2003, I formed my own business with a partner. We worked well together and built the foundations of a good business.

Then came 2010—the beginning of my five-year season of winter in which both my parents fell ill with cancer and I got divorced. During this time, my business partner was approached by another company that wanted to build a succession plan for their senior financial planner. He was roughly ten years older than my partner, who was fourteen years older than me. The company had a huge base of clients and needed our expertise. As overwhelmed as I was with everything in my life at the time it, at first, it was very tempting. We could plug our business into a big, well-oiled machine. We'd have access to a huge number of new clients to serve with terrific resources to support us. This guy would retire someday, and we would run the machine.

As the details of the arrangement were falling into place, I began to feel uneasy, although I didn't know why. If this thing went through, I would make more money and, in many ways, have less stress. All I had to do was serve the clients. I wouldn't be a business owner anymore. I wouldn't have to think about the million things that one does as an entrepreneur. That seemed like a good thing, so I kept going along for the ride.

Right around this same time, I went to my doctor for my annual physical. The nurse practitioner knew me and all the stresses I'd been dealing with. The prior year, she'd encouraged me to take a mild antidepressant and I resisted. This year she was strongly persistent. It's true: I was carrying around some really heavy grief. Though I was working with a therapist to understand and process it all, it was still hard. I was beat down.

I rarely take much medicine or drink much alcohol because my body metabolizes things very quickly, and a little bit goes a long way.[1] But she was insistent, so I agreed to take the medication. I listened to her instructions about the dosage. She told me it might make me feel tired at first. If so, I should take it in the evening instead of the morning.

I tried the medicine for a week, and no matter when I took it, I felt tired. So, I called her back for advice. She said I should take a higher dosage to get past this initial phase. That didn't make sense to me, but I listened. That night I took two of the pills. The next day I woke up with the most extreme sense of apathy I've ever felt in my life. My brain was in a medicated fog. I was alive, but I didn't care about a single thing. Nothing.

I checked my calendar, and since I didn't have any meetings or obligations, I called the office to let them know I wasn't coming in. Then I sat on the couch and played a video game called Halo

---

[1] I want to be absolutely clear that I'm not against taking medication and getting help. I'm not giving advice or making any judgments. I'm simply sharing my experience. Many people have been helped with medication and therapy. I urge you to find what works for you. Ultimately, the medication helped me get to a space that allowed me to make this important decision.

Reach. It's a futuristic war game that I usually wasn't very good at, but in my extreme state of apathy, I also had zero anxiety, and that turned out to be really good for playing the game. I blew away my highest score. But I didn't even care about it. It was the oddest feeling.

Eventually I got off the couch and ate a bit. Sometime in the early afternoon, maybe two or three o'clock, I had the sensation that the medicine wearing off. It felt like fog being burnt off by the morning sun, and I could feel a glimpse of clarity coming. It felt like actual sunshine was coming through that fog of medically induced apathy. I walked down my hallway, and I could sense my awareness, my aliveness fighting to resurface.

I put on my shoes and went out to the park across the street and began walking. As the blood started flowing, the fog kept burning. I walked and walked for more than an hour, and while doing so, my sense of self came back to me. So did the things I was worried or stressed about, but I felt like I could see them from a new perspective.

My thoughts turned to the train I'd felt like I was riding for this business deal. I stopped in my tracks and everything in me said, *I don't want this!* It was loud, clear, final, and certain. Now I knew what had been causing my anxiety and suffering, what was making me uncomfortable. I'd found the sharp pebble in my shoe, and it was coming out ASAP!

> *I stopped in my tracks and everything in me said,* **I don't want this!** *It was loud, clear, final, and certain.*

I didn't want to work for someone else. I didn't want my business partner to suddenly become my boss. We'd been 50/50 partners, and if this deal went through, he'd be my boss. I trusted him, but he would also have bosses who'd tell him what my goals and expectations were. If he wanted to keep them happy, I'd be subject to those demands. I didn't like that.

I'd just gone through the most massive, painful, and expensive changes of my life. My parents were gone. I'd gotten divorced. I was building—figuratively and literally—a new life for my sons and me. We were creating a home that was meaningful, personal, inspiring, and moving. I had a new freedom I'd never known before. And now forces seemed to be moving me toward a corporate job that would suddenly make me subject to company meetings, dress codes, and committee decisions. All for a shortcut to a higher paycheck.

In addition, the week before we'd been in a meeting with some of the senior partners of that firm. It was just before tax time and one of the guys said that he'd been talking to their employees who were doing the taxes and noticed how calm they were. They weren't "stressed enough" to which he declared they had over-staffed. That was the corporate mentality I had almost fallen into. That mentality, which was laughingly approved by the other suits at the table, would be staring at me one day and deciding if my stress levels aligned with their profit goals. No thank you.

It felt like I was being tested. Was I committed to actually living my dreams? Was I committed to truly living on purpose?

YES!

By the end of that walk, I felt extreme clarity. The next day, I told my partner I wasn't interested in anything the other firm had to offer. Thanks, but no thanks. But I understood if he wanted to pursue the opportunity. I'd run all the numbers for my part of the practice, and if my partner left, I'd be fine. I'd have more overhead than I needed, but I could make it work. I was ready to become a solo business owner.

I was becoming more and more aware of what I didn't like about my business. *I'd* changed, but *it* was the same. My partner was the same, but I was evolving. I was stripping off everything that wasn't me and gaining access to the truth of how I wanted to live. As a result, I had a strong and harsh reaction to many of the old things that were still part of my life. My old way of being didn't work any longer. I had co-created this business when I was in my old world—a life of conformity and perpetual compromise. I could now have complete freedom to restructure the business exactly as I wanted. It was like a dam had broken.

Ultimately, my partner decided not to go with the other company, but he wanted to continue on with the status quo. When I presented my ideas for restructuring the business, he didn't want to change anything—which caused me stress. Why would he want anything to be different? I was the one who'd changed, not him. And I didn't want to continue like this.

Friends had encouraged me to turn my furniture-making into a business, and I'd actually explored the economics of it. I looked at studio space. I projected the profit margins and found that the items I made could be sold for quite a profit. But the process had been so fun because there wasn't any pressure surrounding it. It was fun because I could make things the way I wanted to on my own timeline. I didn't want it to become a job. I didn't want to make things for other people. I didn't want to have to sell a table to buy food. If I were financially independent and could make things as art that people could buy or not buy, that would be ideal. But I wasn't going to be a craftsman who had to please the public. That would have robbed me of the joy I'd experienced when I'd done it purely for myself. Making furniture had served its purpose, but now I was moving on.

So I refocused on my financial planning profession and the changes I wanted to make, and becoming my parents' advisor taught me a lot. Both my mom and stepdad had been given a little over a year from the time of their diagnoses until they died, which gave the family time to be with them. It gave me time to help them in many capacities as a son and as a planner, and we had many conversations that wouldn't have happened if they'd been well. The brevity of the time they had left weighed heavily on me. I'd never experienced the death of anyone that close to me before. The more I grew into my new way of being, the more I realized that the real wealth we have are the lessons and memories we pass on.

My curiosity for life had come from my mom. My love of and knowledge of the natural world came to me from her, and from her father who had passed it on to her. When I look into a patch of Missouri woods and see white trees, I'm transported back to my grandfather's car. He pointed a similar patch out to me when I was about five or six.

> *The more I grew into my new way of being, the more I realized that the real wealth we have are the lessons and memories we pass on.*

"See those white trees?" he said. "Those are sycamores. You'll often see them growing in a valley like that because they love water, so you'll find them along creeks."

My awareness of how to make a dollar go further, my sense of play, my drive to learn everything I could had come from my family. Those and a thousand other traits are the wealth of the generations. They're the things that hold us together, make us laugh. My boys share this, and it's why we travel so well together. I'd worked hard to design our lives around our passions and strengths. And I wanted, in some way, to help others do the same. I finally learned that money wasn't the *why* in someone's life; it was a *how*. A tool. We need money, but it's not an end in itself.

My business partner wasn't really interested in the direction I wanted to go, and that was OK. A business partnership is a lot like a marriage; it's a 50/50 arrangement. If one party says no, you either fight or lose.

This felt dreadful to me. I was forty-two years old, and I needed the same level of freedom in my professional world that I had in my personal world. I knew in my heart that my partner and I had to go our separate ways. After many tough conversations, we figured it out.

> **I knew in my heart that my partner and I had to go our separate ways.**

If my personal changes hadn't eventually bled through to my business life, my growth would have been stunted. My freedom restricted. I would have condemned myself to a way of being that was less than whole, and that would have had other negative impacts.

Leaving my business partner to go it alone was another *yes and* turning point. A thousand other moments had brought me to this one, and that pivotal moment led me to deeper and more meaningful relationships with my clients and with my team. It took time and lots of work—something I couldn't have done right out of college. I couldn't have done it if I hadn't already built a business with a good foundation, or if I hadn't developed the skills that I needed to run a successful financial planning practice. At the core, I still do the same thing, but now—because I show up as the truest version of myself possible—I'm a better boss, business owner, and advisor.

The law of unintended consequences is powerful. Everything I've said yes to has splintered into other discoveries that I could never have imagined—things that had bubbled below the surface of my being for years. So, keep listening to your own dreams. Build a plan. Write it down. Take an action. *Yes and . . .*

Building a Tribe

*The fact is that you are a living magnet.
Like iron filings are attracted to a
magnet, you will attract into your life the
people who are in harmony with
your current level of knowledge,
wisdom, and experience.*

~ BRIAN TRACY

WHAT IS A TRIBE? Building your tribe is one of those phrases I hadn't heard about for most of my life, but now it's common. When I first heard the word *tribe*, I thought of a literal tribe of people who lived together in a village, each related to the others. The thing they had most in common was that they were born into the same village.

That's not how we define tribes today. Our tribes consist of the people we most often engage with and spend time with. It's not as literal as having been born in a specific geographic location, but sometimes there's no intentional design behind it. I discovered a fun thing: I could consciously develop my own tribes.

> ### *I discovered a fun thing: I could consciously develop my own tribes.*

My life—and the people who surrounded me when I was married—reflected who I was back then. I didn't have any deep connections because I wasn't deeply connected with myself, which didn't concern me because that's how I'd always been. But when I went through several crises and experienced real changes in my life, I saw the depth—or the lack of it—in my connections.

I noticed how many people, who were fine and lovely individuals, were simply extras in my story, just as I was in theirs. The people who didn't get me. Who saw me as just one of many people who are "like us." Who does the things we do. Thinks the things we think, such as, *This is what work means. This is where we take vacations, how we cut our hair, how we dress, what we do on weekends or after work.* My tribe was full of banal and meaningless conversations like, "Did you see the game?" and "It sure is hot/cold."

A tribe has a collective vision of what "we" do, and when you're in a structure that you haven't consciously chosen, it's hard to extract yourself and live the way you want to. I don't blame my old tribe for not getting me. How could they have known me when I didn't know myself? I was living a half-life version of myself, which is what I projected to them.

As I've changed and grown in ways that are still somewhat shocking to me, my tribe has also evolved. It changed from people who happened to be in my life because I lived near them or their kids went to school with mine to a rapidly evolving expanse of people who—like iron files—were pulled into my world. My tribe is an eclectic mix of people who reflect my interests, passions, and values.

Some have been healers, like my therapists. Others have been coaches who nudged me onto the path that I'm still on. I worked with professional coaches to help me look at my business differently. I engaged a team that helps me stay physically fit. They helped me recover from knee surgery and continue to help me with my goal of staying healthy, fit, and strong.

My tribe is an eclectic mix of people who reflect my interests, passions, and values.

And then there's my improv team. I love each of them in a way I never felt in my old life. We practice on Sundays from 6:00 p.m. to 8:00 p.m. Before, Sundays always felt a little down because it was the day before the school and work week started. But for the past four years, I've had something really fun to look forward to on Sundays. And that makes a difference in how I feel all day on Sunday because I know I'll see my friends at the end of the day.

On Sunday nights, we dive into this fun, weird art form that we all love. We get to laugh and play together. To be real and vulnerable together. We're there to love and support each other, and that's an amazing thing I never experienced in my old life.

For more than two years I've spent my Friday or Saturday mornings with my teacher and friend, Valentina, who teaches me Italian. She introduced me to her friend, Rosanna, with whom I've spent many hours on Skype, helping her brush up on her English while I practice my Italian.

My tribe has expanded to so many varied groups whose Venn diagrams overlap with mine in a way that's mutually beneficial. As my tribe has grown, so has my ability to politely and respectfully remove myself from people and situations that don't feel healthy. I don't need to chase anyone or work to be in anyone's life. The old Carlo was insecure. I was a huge people-pleaser who allowed people to be unkind or impolite to me. I don't do that anymore. I am happy. I am whole. The people who are in my life are there because I want them to be. When I sense someone trying to change or judge me, I walk away without the fear of being alone.

> *As my tribe has grown, so has my ability to politely and respectfully remove myself from people and situations that don't feel healthy.*

As I've gained greater clarity about who I am, that clarity has driven my actions and given me confidence to say yes and try new things, which activates the magnet. When we dive into the things we love, we attract like-minded people with whom we share mutual values and interests.

My first trip alone—in 2013—gave me a first-hand experience with this. My divorce was finalized in 2012, and I felt the pull to be in nature, but I didn't have the strength or will to do the planning. I'd heard that REI had a travel company, so I perused their website. They offered what I came to think of as adult summer camp/adventure experiences—excursions all over the world.

I could pick the region, the length of time, and the type and rigor of activity I wanted. There was a week-long hiking excursion through the Austrian Alps that caught my eye. But I'd just gotten divorced and didn't have the time or money for that. So, I kept looking and found a volunteer section on the website. I found a four-day trip to Yosemite that involved doing trail maintenance. That sounded perfect to me.

I signed up. I downloaded a list of things to bring for camping and instructions about where to go and when to report in. I was soon on my way. Yosemite is quite crowded most of the year, but this was in the Fall, so it was more lightly populated. Plus, we got to use a special campsite for volunteers that felt private. I didn't know a soul, but I quickly made friends. People of all ages from around the US and a few from other countries were there— roughly twenty-five people wanted to spend their vacation time working in Yosemite. After we received instructions about how to avoid being eaten by bears, we set up our tents and settled in.

They provided hot breakfasts and dinners via a food truck that also had everything we needed to pack a good lunch. Each morning, we'd get up and eat together under the trees. That cool morning pine air never got old!

Then our leaders drove us to the place we'd be working that day. We spent most of our time on the John Muir Trail raking, moving fallen rocks, and shoring up the trail where it had washed out. We greeted hikers as they made their way up and down the trails. The days were full of hard work, but they didn't seem long.

This group was my tribe for that short time. For those few days, we quickly became a *we*. We were fixing this trail. We were helping each other and the hikers who were trekking toward Glacier Point. People from all over the world stopped and thanked us or asked us what we were doing and why. We worked, talked, laughed, joked, played, and accomplished a lot.

In the evenings, even though we were exhausted, we social- ized around the campfire. One night we even played a bunch of short-form improv games. People were curious about improv, and they were eager to try it out, so we played. Men, women, people from across the US, and even other countries. People ranging in age from their twenties to their sixties playing under the stars and trees around the campfire. Laughing and playing in the woods like a tribe that existed before the modern world. In that moment, for those four days, we were a tribe. We ate together, slept in our tents in a shared space in the woods, and worked hard each day for a purpose beyond ourselves. We each arrived with our own intentions from great distances, and then, when it was over, we left each other.

That was six years ago. Some of us became Facebook friends, and we follow each other's adventures, but I haven't seen any of them in person since, and that's OK. The experience taught me how to quickly find and meet people by simply engaging in my passions. Many people are searching for the same meaning as I am, and when I follow my passions and say yes, we find each other.

My tribe of people near and far help me learn and grow. When I find others who are into the things that light me up, it reinforces my passions. Then I get to cross-fertilize the various groups with my experiences. My tribe is a living entity that expands far and wide. In any given week, I check in and engage with friends all over the country and around the world. I didn't even know many of my best friends five years ago.

> *The experience taught me how to quickly find and meet people by simply engaging in my passions.*

And I feel even more connected to the people who are still a part of my world from my previous life because as I've emerged—as I've learned to speak and live my truth—they stayed with me. The things I was afraid to admit or reveal about myself ended up enriching my life and those relationships.

It's so important not to condemn or judge the people in your life for holding you back. They aren't the ones holding you back, you are. They are simply a reflection of how you see yourself. Like a magnet, you draw people and circumstances to yourself, so if you aren't happy with either, then *you* must be the one to change.

Chapter
ELEVEN

_____ Is Not My Therapy

*The cave you fear to enter
holds the treasure you seek.*
~ JOSEPH CAMPBELL

SIMPLY THINKING ABOUT GOING to a psychologist would have been impossible for me at an earlier time in my life. I would have felt too vulnerable. At first, I felt ashamed about going. Like I'd given up. Like I'd lost my struggle to go it alone. All the books on self-help and success had claimed that I could will my way to success. That I could fake it until I made it. That I could be just as happy as I decided to be. If it was going to be, it was up to me. These books reinforced the macho, solo, strong individual stereotype. I believed in self-reliance and hard work, and I believed in discipline and focus, but going to therapy wasn't about any of those things.

For some, there's still a stigma about going to therapy, which is one of the reasons I'm so open in talking about it. Had anyone I loved or trusted explained what it was all about or how I could benefit from it, I would have been more eager to try it. But, sadly, I'd never heard anyone talk about going to therapy. With no support or guidance, I put my head down and pushed and pushed and pushed—until life broke me open.

I've heard so many people say that (fill in the blank) is my therapy.

Running is my therapy.
Yoga is my therapy.
Nature is my therapy.
Shopping is my therapy.

Those activities and a million more can certainly be therapeutic, stress relieving, and relaxing—and they're important to a healthy life—but they aren't the same as engaging in therapy. So _____ is not my therapy, and it's not yours either.

My addiction to hard work was celebrated and cheered. What if I'd been smoking or doing drugs? Then society would have frowned on me and told me to quit, to just say no. It's as if your means of dealing with your fears, stressors, anxiety, or whatever is eating at you is seen as unhealthy, then stop. Get rid of it. If it's socially acceptable, then it's good for you!

But is it? How do you feel about the thought of your "therapy" going away? How would you feel if you lost your yoga, your running, your shopping, or whatever you run to when you feel stressed or down to get that rush of endorphins or burn away your anxiety?

TRIGGER WARNING: If you're having a strong negative reaction to the idea of therapy, then you're probably exactly where I was. So please take a deep breath and stay with me.

Before the winter of my life, the time when everything fell apart, yoga was my therapy. Specifically, hot yoga. I discovered it a couple years after my younger son was born. I'd hurt my back while lifting drywall during yet another episode of my "This Old House" phase of life. Up to that point, I'd stayed fairly active with sports and exercise. Even when I was young, if I was stressed, I'd do pushups, sit ups, run, lift weights, or go kick a soccer ball to diffuse my energy—to burn it out of me, so I could relax. It was instinctual, and I found it very helpful. When I stumbled across yoga, it had the same effect. In some ways it was even better than going to the gym because I could totally unplug in a class setting.

When a class started, I felt like I was strapped into a roller coaster, and I could almost hear the *clink, clink, clink* of it pulling up the first hill. In those moments I might still be stressed about something from my personal or work life, but once we crested that first hill, I'd have to focus on my breathing. This was hot yoga— ninety minutes in an inferno of 100+ degrees with who-knows-what kind of heat index when you factored in the humidity. If I didn't focus on my breathing, I'd get winded and feel overheated and dizzy. I'd be miserable. Or rather, I wouldn't be able to endure the misery. I felt like I was in a crucible and could feel the stress and tension from my incongruent life melt away. But that was my delusion. I wasn't fixing or addressing any of the causes . . . I was releasing a pressure valve to get through another day.

As my yoga practice improved, I came to appreciate the meditative aspect of it. In class, we were asked to stand on one foot and grab the other to do the standing splits—and all kinds of things I'd never thought to try before. I realized that, unlike going to the gym or any other exercise I'd done before, that if I wasn't absolutely present, I couldn't balance on one foot. If I was in the middle of a posture and I thought about work or money or anything other than that present moment, I fell out of the posture. There's nothing wrong with falling out; you just jump back in again. But you only have a short time for each posture. Before you know it, the teacher says, "and change," and it's over.

> *I wasn't fixing or addressing any of the causes . . . I was releasing a pressure valve to get through another day.*

So, I learned to be present in a way I never understood before. I learned to really, really relax and to still my mind. The biggest breakthrough came when I finally learned to do a handstand. When I was young, I always had the strength to stand on my hands if I was supported, and I could easily walk on my hands. But I could never stand still and balance on my hands. One day I took a workshop with Esak, an amazing individual and a great yoga teacher who travels the world teaching others how to improve their practice. He instructed us to stand on our feet, close our eyes, and simply notice ourselves standing. He said to notice all the micro adjustments that our feet, ankles, and legs made as we stood.

"When most people try to stand on their hands," he said, "they lock their elbows, which makes it much harder because all the work is focused in the wrists and hands." He encouraged us to seek the same stance when we were standing on our hands that we had while standing on our feet.

I went to work, and within a week I got it. Something clicked and I could stand on my hands just as easily as on my feet. Just like balancing on one leg, I had to clear my mind—but to an even greater degree. When I balanced on my hands, my brain felt clear. Like water. It was a peace I'd never before experienced, and what a strange way to achieve it! I became an even stronger believer in yoga as a way for me to not only relieve stress but to focus and clear my mind. I was practically addicted to it.

You've seen the t-shirts that say Know Yoga, Know Peace. No Yoga, No Peace. That was me. I used yoga to get my fix of peace and clarity. It not only helped me burn through stress, but it also helped me reach calming states of consciousness. I could let go and find peace on the mat. But the next day, the stress of life would compound, and I'd feel panicky if I couldn't go within. I obsessed about getting back in the studio to get my fix. I'd feel relief that night after class, but the pressure and anxiety would start building again the next day.

Yoga wasn't actually my therapy; it was a form of self-medication. I used it to burn through the stress that coursed through me. It helped me find respite. It was therapeutic, but it didn't help me get to the root cause of my distress. It was like taking ibuprofen for a headache without realizing the headache was due to dehydration.

Oddly, this type of addiction is celebrated because it's considered healthy. I was fit and strong physically, but I was medicating and masking my pain with yoga. And no one at the time could have convinced me of this. I found something that made me feel great—a cure—and I would have vehemently defended my addiction to it. I loved yoga and encouraged everyone to join me in my drug of choice—until it was snatched away.

> *Yoga wasn't actually my therapy;*
> *it was a form of self-medication.*

I travelled to San Diego to take a yoga seminar, a really intense week-long event with two sessions per day. If something makes you feel that good, then more is better, right? If three or four times a week felt good, why not do it twice a day for a week?!

It was quite an experience to be in a giant room with a couple hundred amazingly fit people all doing this thing we loved together. It was challenging and exhausting, but I loved it. I was in a community of people with the same obsession. We were all there for our own reasons, but everyone was there to push themselves.

Then my knee started feeling odd. No pain, just *off*. After class, I walked back to my hotel room, and it felt really funny. It had an odd clicking/clunking sensation. It didn't hurt, but it felt like my knee was falling apart. Fortunately, it was the end of the week. I limped through the airport. Limped home. Limped to a doctor. Limped to get a second opinion. Limped to a surgeon and got my torn meniscus fixed. The doctor said it was likely due to the wear and tear from playing soccer years ago. Regardless of the source, I was about to dive into a healing process that I wasn't prepared for—and it was painful.

But the pain wasn't from the surgery. It was from not getting my medicine. My drug of choice. My fix into bliss. My yoga. I had to rest to heal, and resting meant that all my stress, unhappiness, and unresolved shadows were right there, swirling like a tornado inside me. I was like a kid at a birthday party who wasn't normally allowed to eat sugar but consumes massive amounts of punch and cake, and then the monster emerges. My years of sweating, stretching, running, and lifting weights had done *zero* to make me aware of my shadow. Zero to help me understand the source of my stress and unhappiness. Nothing to help me look at my situation in order to learn and grow. If anything, doing yoga had buried my troubles even deeper. Years and years of pain was bottled up inside me. A deep river that had no outlet.

My stepdad had just died, and I was nearing the end of my marriage. I carried the trauma from my childhood and my parent's divorce. All those years, exercise had been my way to relieve stress, but it did nothing to heal me internally. It hadn't made me more conscious, more awake, more aware, or more whole. I was an addict, and someone had flushed my stash. No yoga, no peace. I was a mess.

> *I had to rest to heal, and resting meant that all my stress, unhappiness, and unresolved shadows were right there, swirling like a tornado inside me.*

I finally decided to get therapy. Real, deep therapy.

For me, therapy was the process of shining a light on the things I hadn't seen—or didn't want to see. It was holding up a mirror and finally seeing myself. To see the role I'd played in building the life I was living. To see what I'd refused to look at before. And over time, I began to build a skill set that would allow me to do this for myself.

During the worst of this grief, I had absolutely no energy or any interest in exercise. Dealing with multiple deaths and my divorce had sucked the life out of me. My therapy shined the light on shadow within me, and I did the hard work. I looked at the role my wounds and shadows had played in building my life, but it was almost too much for me to handle. The only thing that kept me going was my role as a father. I would never let anything slide with my boys.

When I started feeling better, I thought I should start exercising again, but I couldn't do it. One day I finally put it into words—I now had an aversion to exercise. I couldn't get myself to do it anymore.

It was my sadness, grief, and stress that had driven my compulsion for physical activity. As I was healing and growing, I no longer felt that stress, but when I tried to exercise, I either couldn't do it or it would trigger the memories and feelings I'd had when I was so miserable. My subconscious associated my unhappy state with exercise. I had used my negative inner emotions to drive that physical activity and to push myself to the point of hurting myself. And now I couldn't do it anymore.

The rational part of me knew that exercise was good for me, that I needed it for the health of my body but not to burn away unhappiness. It wasn't like I'd been abusing some substance that was harmful or even illegal. I was *exercising*. I'd been fit during that time, but now I had a layer of what I called divorce fat around my gut! What the heck?!

I needed to rewire my relationship with exercise, so I decided to get help, and it started with my knee. Three years after my surgery, my knee still didn't feel right. After a few months of post-op rehab, I'd been discharged and had started to deal with the fires in my life. I was in the middle of my crises, so not having full range of motion in my knee wasn't a high priority.

But three years later, I'd had enough. I went to a rehab center to work with sports rehab specialists. After six months, I was cleared by the physical therapist and doctor to start strength training. I'd had such a great experience with them that I signed up for strength, exercise, and nutritional coaching.

For two years, I went to their facility a few times a week and did whatever they told me for that hour. They asked questions about my nutrition, hydration, stress levels, and rest. I didn't quite understand why I needed someone to tell me what to do, but it was working. I began to feel better, gain muscle, and lose some of that divorce fat. After a few months, my thoughts had become clearer. I was eating better and staying active. And this form of exercise didn't have any of the negative connections to my past, so I wasn't haunted by ghosts that sabotaged my workouts.

At this point, I'd started to travel and was gone too much to take advantage of the in-house training, so I signed up for a program where they prepared my workouts based on my needs. Once a month, I went in to learn the new program, and then I did the workouts on my own while I was in Florence, Chicago, San Francisco, and many other cities. Most gyms let me buy a day or week pass, and it was fun to visit new gyms. I found a new way to connect with physical activity for the purpose of staying healthy, and it was no longer my means to avoid facing my shadows.

The psychological therapy was healing, not addictive. I liked it, appreciated it, and grew from it, but I never panicked at the thought of it going away. I stopped going regularly a few years ago, but I still check in now and then when I have questions or want another opinion. If I ever feel like I need more than that, I won't hesitate to go, but I don't need it to feel at peace.

I now have a regular exercise regime that keeps me healthy, strong, and fit, and it has a huge host of ancillary benefits. But on their own, lifting weights, practicing yoga, or going for a walk don't have the same benefits as doing shadow work with a qualified therapist.

I still hear people say that _____ is my therapy. I don't judge or suggest that you stop doing a healthy activity that makes you feel good and probably comes with a tribe of people who support you. But I do offer my experience to encourage you to dive into your own growth and self-discovery.

I'm actually glad that I hurt my knee. I'm glad my drug was snatched away because it had blocked my escape. Getting help during the worst of times helped me immensely, but the most powerful growth came when I proactively looked, with the help of a therapist, to see what lay beneath the surface and to face my fears.

TWELVE

I Said to Myself . . .

The world is given to me only once, not
one existing and one perceived.
Subject and object are only one.

~ ERWIN SCHRÖDINGER

IF YOU'VE MADE IT THIS FAR, then something must be resonating with you. Stick with me, take in a big belly breath, and let's go to the deep end of the pool.

I've already mentioned meditation a few times. It's something that's always interested me, and for many years I tried it here and there but didn't understood what it was, how to do it, or what could come from it. In college, I read what I could on the subject, and I even went to group meditation events over the years to learn more, but there was never any instruction. I had no context for what I was trying to do, so I had a nice experience, nothing else.

My experiences often ended up in the woo-woo category of mysticism, which wasn't what I was seeking. Like the feeling I got after a yoga class or a walk in the woods, it was therapeutic and relaxing, and that was beneficial, but it didn't provide lasting change. The impermanence of it was frustrating. The irony is that I was searching, seeking, and reaching for something that was always right there with me. Even as I write this, I realize how frustratingly cliché that may sound. It always did to me until something clicked.

While I'm not a trained expert, a guru, or an authority on this subject, the most profound means of growth has been for me to combine a meditation practice—and the things that come from it—with shadow work. Regardless of what you do or don't believe in, this can help you. I promise.

Let's start with a story I heard some time back, although I don't recall the source: One day a wave rose up out of the deep, blue ocean. From its height, it could look out over the ocean and see an expanse of other waves. Ah! So beautiful! It loved some of those waves dearly. Others, it tried to avoid. Some didn't even notice the wave, and that hurt and felt sad. *How can I feel connected? the wave asked. Where do my loved ones go when they disappear? Do they return to their source, or God, the universe, or whatever there is? How can I connect with my source? How can I feel whole?*

How silly, right? How could a wave *not* be connected to its source? It literally sits on top of it. Its very nature is an aspect of its source. One cannot scoop a wave up in a bucket and still call the thing in a bucket a wave any more than one can have a bucket of carbon, iron, water, and whatever else we are physically made of and call it me or you. Whatever it is that is us transcends our physical self. Even if you don't believe in or accept anything spiritual, whatever that energy is transcends our physical atoms. We, like a wave, are energy that is in a constantly changing mass of matter. Spirit in motion. Whatever spirit means to you.

Imagine a movie of a person's physical self—condensed down to a one-minute time lapse. From a tiny baby to an elderly man or woman rising, cresting, and falling before your eyes. When the energy of that person is gone, the matter disappears back into the earth. Our physical atoms are in a constant state of change and renewal. Roughly every seven years, we have a completely new body. Pull out a picture of yourself from seven years or more ago. Whatever it is that's you remembers this moment, but not a single atom in your physical body exists now that existed then.

Like the energy rolling through the ocean that manifests as a wave that skirts the big blue expanse so, too, are we an energy that transcends our physical selves. Constantly renewing with new physical matter and leaving the old behind. We adopted a small "i am," which is how each of us refers to ourselves. When people are asked to describe themselves they jump into: my name is, I'm a man/woman, I'm this old, I'm this tall, my hair is this color, I give away chunks of my life each day to do this thing for money, and that's what I am; these are my roles in life and that is what I am; I have these kinds of things, I live in this zip code and that's what I am; I have this degree from this school and that's what I am. These words are scribbled on a business card and that's what I AM.

> *Like the energy rolling through the ocean that manifests as a wave that skirts the big blue expanse so, too, are we an energy that transcends our physical selves.*

Really? That's what you are? Why? How do you know? Because one day you woke up, and people began telling you who and what you are? Who were you before you knew your name? Who are you if you forget it? Dr. Wayne Dyer warned not to be what you do because then if you stop doing, you'll stop being. People go through all kinds of existential crises because of this very thing. Jumping out of buildings because of a stock market crash is an extreme example of this. For those people, their identity was their portfolio. Their net worth. When it vanished, they threw themselves into the abyss because they were "ruined." If you start with nothing, then are you starting from ruin? Many people wither and die shortly after retirement because they don't have an identity outside of what they thought they were as an employee, executive, professional, or however they sold their time and life to get money.

If you feel yourself tightening up or wanting to defend that you really *are* the senior manager of XYZ, you really *are* the president of this or that, then take a breath and come a little deeper.

After a major life change, a crisis could have you asking, "Who am I now that I lost this job, this marriage, my youth, my house, my health, my portfolio, my whatever?" When we define ourselves by and limit ourselves to external, temporal things we are setting ourselves up for pain.

So, who are you? Regardless of your spiritual beliefs, even if you don't have any, right now there's an aspect of you that's the witness of everything that arises in your consciousness. It was there on the day of your birth, there on your first day of kindergarten, there for graduation, there when you fell in love, there when your heart was broken, there in sickness and health, there for all the happy, sad, scary, and lovely moments of your life. Anything you are aware of is an object that is not you; it is an object of the awareness that *is* you. The witness that saw those things. That hears your thoughts. That sees your dreams. You are the one witnessing whatever is happening in that dream, just as you are witnessing all that is arising for you right now.

So, who are you?

Right now, I'm aware that my fingers are typing the words that appear on my laptop screen. I'm aware of the slight discomfort in my elbows as they rest on the table in the coffeeshop where I'm working. I'm aware of the noise in the café. The smell of the food, the music that is struggling to be heard over it all. There's a sensation of stress in my chest, neck, and shoulders from the slight anxiety from too many stimuli, or perhaps too much cold brew. This is what I've turned into my meditation. Not sitting and trying to "become," but sitting and being the observer. I've learned to rest in this *witnessing awareness.*

Right now, look at the objects that are near you. A book, a tree, a desk, a chair, a coffee cup, something outside of you. It's so easy to recognize this as *not you.* All those things are objects you are aware of. You can hold or touch or see each thing that is not you. This thing is an object of your awareness. You are not this thing; it's the object of your awareness. If you are aware of it, how could it be you? You are that which is aware. The thing is the object of that awareness.

The beauty of this mental shift is that it doesn't require a meditation room, a meditation mat or pillow, or any of the things usually associated with the practice of meditation. You can embrace it right now wherever you are, doing whatever you're doing because it's with you right now, always and forever. When you're attached to your titles and roles and the incessant chatter in your mind that continually plays a movie of the past things you should either regret, be sad about, or miss, you feel a jolt of pain. Or if you play a movie of the coming attractions of what you should worry about, be scared of, or feel angry about, you again feel that jolt of pain.

"How can I let *that* go?!" you ask. "*That* is me!"

Let me explain. It's easy to see that this book is not you, but rather the object of your awareness. But what about your thoughts and feelings?

Right now, stop reading for a minute. Sit in silence. What do you hear? Do you hear talking? Do you hear words bubbling up in your mind? Do you see images? Every moment you're aware of the chatter, you identify the chatter as if it was you. You notice the thoughts. You hear the words in your head. You notice the anxiety, stress, happiness. If you're aware of it, it is not you. Anything you're aware of is the object of your awareness. There's something that's seeing and something seen. Something that's noticing the feeling or the energy. The closer it is to you, the more resistance you'll have in letting go of that being you. If you can't look at a thought, feeling, or emotion now, you will eventually be able to with time.

It's easy to look back at a younger version of yourself as an object. Think of something you used to do that you'd never do now. You can look back objectively at your old self and say, "I can't believe I used to do that!" Or say that. Think that. Feel that. That old self no longer seems like you; you've distanced yourself from *that* person.

"What's the point of all this?" you ask. "Why bother? I'm not into this!"

I've had these same arguments with myself, so let me tell you what I've learned from this shift to becoming an observer versus accepting my thoughts and feelings as being *me*.

Stepping into witnessing awareness has accelerated my growth now versus waiting for years to have the benefit of distance and perspective. Being able look at myself now, at my feelings now, my stress now, my happiness or sadness now, saves me the pain of waiting for years and years to change and then having an insight when it's not as helpful because the change has already occurred. But it's constant practice. It's easy to fall out of that space and back into the chatter and emotions that can be a roller coaster. And like a roller coaster, it can be fun, exhilarating, and scary, or stressful.

Remember the story I shared about my brother telling me I wasn't myself in my marriage? Remember what I told you about the observations that my therapists and other friends shared with me? These things hit me so hard because I already knew them deep down, yet I was too close to see them. Stepping into witnessing awareness gives you that space now. Let me share a recent example from a tool I learned from Ken Wilber's teachings.

> *These things hit me so hard because I already knew them deep down, yet I was too close to see them.*

I moved offices earlier this year. I moved into a smaller, temporary office suite while a new space was being built across town. The new office was in the same building as my old office, so it wasn't a big move. It was a good opportunity to get rid of things I didn't need or want anymore, and I knew this temporary space was a stepping-stone to where I really wanted to be. And I was saving money with a lease that was super flexible with a really cool landlord. All wins, right?

The move occurred between Christmas and the New Year. As my company settled into our temporary space, I started feeling depressed. I felt sad, but I didn't know why. I felt so dragged down that I actually got sick. Not lay-in-bed sick, but I'd gotten the kind of cold that bounces around humanity when we're all stuck indoors because it's cold outside. To make things worse, it got dark at 4:30. I felt off for nearly two months and took decongestants to get through the things I needed to do in life.

One day, I recognized my sadness as something different from simply not feeling good. This practice of learning to rest in my awareness was something I'd been pursuing, and I reminded myself to look at the sadness. So, I sat in meditation and felt the sadness. As I sat with it and breathed, I reminded myself that I was aware of the sadness. I could feel it in me and on me. Because I was aware of it, the sadness was not me. I was that which was aware of it, resting in the feeling of observation. Literally saying "I am aware of this sadness. Because I am aware of it, it is not me. I am that which is aware of it. Aware of the feeling. Aware of the effect it is having on me."

As I did this, I could feel the heaviness lift off me. I could feel myself looking it. It wasn't *me*. With this space between the feeling and my witnessing awareness I could understand why I was sad. I wasn't sad to be in Suite 40 versus Suite 200. I wasn't sad to be on the east versus the west side of the building. With that moment of space separated from the feeling, I understood that I was sad because my office had been the last physical space that hadn't changed since my divorce. Since the death of my parents.

The desk I'd gotten rid of was an inexpensive piece of pressboard furniture I'd purchased from Office Depot twenty-two years ago—when my first son was on his way into this world. I didn't need the desk anymore, and I hadn't sat at it to work in over two years. But I had sat at that desk with Alex next to me in a pumpkin seat, looking up at me playing with his toys. Later when I started my own business, I moved that desk from my home to my office. I'd built my business at that desk, taking it from the days when I sometimes had to write personal checks to pay the rent— which meant that I didn't get a paycheck that month—to a place where it supported me in a way that allowed me to live the life I wanted. I'd sat at that desk with countless clients and helped them through huge life decisions. New marriages, new babies, divorces, deaths, retirement, and so much more. I'd sat at that desk and had countless heavy conversations with my mom during my stepdad's sickness and her own. I'd sat there as my mom's son, financial planner, and executor of her estate as I went through the ugly process of deconstructing her world after her death. Paying bills, closing accounts, arguing with the cable company about closing her account, so I'd stop getting bills from them months after her death. And I'd sat there as I made important decisions about my own divorce—and even my business divorce.

> *I understood that I was sad because my office had been the last physical space that hadn't changed since my divorce. Since the death of my parents.*

I'd stopped using the desk a couple years ago and started working at a conference table, so I could get used to working remotely. I wanted to prove to myself that I didn't need a regular desk or even an office, and I did that. When it was time to move, I didn't want to bring the desk with me because I didn't need that piece of furniture anymore. So, I donated it without any obvious emotion . . . until it hit me.

I was amazed at how quickly this all flooded into my mind, simply because I gave myself space to look at the emotion. I wasn't in a full-scale state of depression, I just felt sad and didn't know why. Creating this space allowed me to recognize it. Once I saw it, I allowed it to settle in. I took time to journal and think about the loss I was feeling.

I could have just gone for a run, taken a vacation, or bought some new shiny thing to give me a rush of endorphins or some sense of peacefulness. But that wouldn't have afforded me any insight or growth. I would have tackled the symptom, not the cause. The root of my mild depression was that I needed to acknowledge my grieving for a workspace and desk that held so many memories—the final physical space that had remained the same since my divorce. Now I could see that I'd held onto that desk way longer than I needed to because of all the emotional attachments. The desk was a cheap desk that had been moved at least six times. It wasn't a family heirloom, and it certainly wasn't something anyone would want because of its own value or crafts-manship. But there were memories and emotions tied to it that I hadn't recognized. A shadow that kept it in my life.

When the desk was gone, the shadow surfaced as unresolved mourning with such ferocity that it wore me down until I felt exhausted and sick. Now, I quietly reminded myself that I was not that sadness. I was aware of the sadness; therefore I was that which was aware. This gave me the perspective to look at it as if it were someone else's problem, and with that space, I gained an objec-tivity that also delivered all my memories and emotions to help me see things clearly. Now I was doing in one session what used to take several while working with a therapist. At a minimum, I was working through my shadows at a much quicker pace. Sometimes I can do this all alone and gain great insight; sometimes I'll check back with my therapist to talk it through.

This tool can help give you that perspective now. Help you learn and grow from your feelings now. Help you look at the feel-ing, then trace it back to a source that may be a deep rabbit hole of shadows you can work through. And, most profoundly, you can step into and be aware of the energy and spirit that is *you* skirting across an ocean of God, or whatever you choose to call it. If we are an energy surging through matter like a wave, and we call that energy spirit, then like the wave and the ocean "there is only Spirit, there is only God, there is only Emptiness in all its radiant wonder. All the good and all the evil, the very best and the very worst, the upright and the degenerate-each and all are radically perfect manifestations of Spirit precisely as they are. There is nothing but God, nothing but the Goddess, nothing but Spirit in all directions, and not a grain of sand, not a speck of dust, is more or less Spirit than any other."[2]

I told you it was the deep end of the pool. Whatever you do or don't believe, this is what stepping into your witnessing awareness can open up for you. Now lets head back to the other side of the pool.

> ### *I was aware of the sadness; therefore I was that which was aware.*

On a more practical level, learning to identify with the witness of your emotions and states is also really helpful in stressful situations. You've probably had things happen that were terrible or stressful or scary at the time, but years later you laughed about it. You can learn to do that now.

For example, when I'm in traffic and something starts to stress me out, I can feel the tension rising in me. I can feel it in my whole body. But when I take a breath and remind myself that I am not that stress, I am that which is aware of it, I can feel the stress melt off me. I feel clarity return to my thoughts and my heart slows down. I take my system out of the fight-or-flight mode, which has terrible effects on my health. Even if you have zero spiritual beliefs, surely you recognize the adverse effects that cortisol has on your system over time and can find a use for witnessing awareness.

This isn't something you do once and then you're done. It's a practice. It takes time, and as you practice it will make more sense. I hope you'll give it a try and use it as part of your process of waking up.

---

[2] Ken Wilber, "Always Already," in The Eye of Spirit: An Integral Vision for a World Gone Slightly Mad, Boulder: Shambhala Publications, 2001.

Chapter
THIRTEEN

Waking Up from the American Dream

You come into this world with nothing and you go empty-handed. The wealth of life lies in how you allow its experiences to enrich you.

~ SADHGURU

BEFORE I WENT THROUGH my massive changes, I held myself back—both mentally and emotionally. I'd built a life-style that was, itself, a barrier to the way I really wanted to live. But over the past few years, I've restructured my life to give myself the freedom of time and money. I continually evaluate how I want to spend my time and who I want to spend it with, and I eliminate anything that doesn't fit. I had to make these necessary changes in order to live the life I want.

With my parents' deaths came a stark revelation that time was a limited resource, as was money. As I deconstructed their physical world—selling, giving away, and disposing of so much stuff—I saw what my own future looked like if I didn't change. I remembered what they'd said about the things they wanted to do but "never had time," or "never got around to it," or couldn't because of stuff that had to be done. Things had to be cleaned, fixed, and fed.

My response was to free up my time and money, so I could pursue the life I wanted to live. Time and again, I see Americans living in a cult of busy, trapped by their commitments of time and expense. I wanted relief from that.

> *I continually evaluate how I want to spend my time and who I want to spend it with, and I eliminate anything that doesn't fit.*

When I graduated college, I began reading self-help and motivational books by all the popular authors. I was excited to read and learn from them and was motivated and inspired by the idea that I could do, have, or be whatever I wanted. I was twenty-something years old, and for my whole life I'd felt a lack of financial security, due to my parents' divorce and the struggles my mom endured financially.

I had a lack of money shadow, and I was convinced that I could fill that with the American Dream. I wrote down my dreams of having a ginormous house in a beautiful neighborhood with acres of land, and a library, and meditation room, and maybe a second home and enough money to retire someday—and on and on and on. (I found one of those notebooks from twenty years ago and buried in that list was *learn Italian*. That obviously took a back burner as I gave my life away for my stuff.) I attacked this goal with an energy that exhausts me now to think about it.

I constantly read and listened to books about success, motivation, goal setting, and time management. I dove in hard and followed the advice of the authors. I woke up early, read, studied, and went to work. I worked long hours, listened to books commuting to and from work, then I came home and studied more in the evening. When I wasn't reading about success, I was studying to master my profession.

At age twenty-four, I was already married and was a father. I'd fully bought into the idea that more was better, so I launched right into the path of our modern serf system. What's that you ask? Well, let me explain. When I started my family, I did all the things one "has to" do. I bought a house (debt), I bought a car so I could go to work (debt), bought another car for my wife, so she could work and get around during the day with Alex (debt), and we filled our home with all things a home is supposed to have. Appliances, furniture, lawn equipment, tools to fix the house (more money).

I woke up every Monday and left my wife and son to go to an office to make money that we would then send off to a multitude of banks, hoping to earn enough to save for our future. My time and money were already spent each day—before I went out to earn it. Our first home was, indeed, a starter home, and it was just fine. In fact, it was the home I grew up in. My mom had sold it to us and gave us a good deal because it had thirty years of deferred maintenance that needed to be rectified. My wife and I worked hard to fix up that house and make it our home. Thousands of dollars and countless hours later, it was done.

Time was flying by, and now Alex was three years old. He would start school in two years, so choosing a school district weighed on us. And we wanted to be closer to the things we liked to do in our city. Since everyone else liked doing those things too, that meant we were looking at a more expensive zip code. In order to afford it, we bought a charming old home in a turn-of-the-last-century town—that had over fifty years of deferred maintenance. It also had that much bigger yard I'd dreamed about.

I was making more money now and had learned so much about renovating homes that I was excited about diving into this project, and I did! My dreams and goals were all around having a lovely home and a big yard, and I was doing it. But the cost was more than I bargained for, in terms of money and the life I gave away.

We worked and worked and worked to make this house a home. The first big project was to build a patio. I had to tear out the old patio that was built in the 1950s, excavate a fifteen-by-thirty-foot area, fill that in with gravel, sand, then stone for paving—and build a retaining wall. I started in the spring, and it took most of the summer.

> *But the cost was more than I bargained for, in terms of money and the life I gave away.*

That was just the beginning! Bathrooms, kitchen, refinishing hardwood floors, paint, tile—my time and money were consumed by that house. For days, weeks, months, and years I gave my time and money to the house, to cars, to stuff.

The more money I made, the more there was to do. I saved what I could along the way and began building a nest egg for retirement and my boys' education, but the goal line never felt any closer. The gap was always bigger. The more I earned, the more I needed to earn. Even when we didn't have projects for the house, we spent thousands of dollars each year just to keep it up. Fixing and replacing all our stuff—cars, lawnmowers, appliances—all of it constantly demanded my time and money and, thus, my life.

You might wonder why I did all the work myself instead of hiring people. I'd learned in economics class about the division of labor and that it would be more efficient for me to hire an expert, so I could go do what I excelled at. But I wasn't an hourly employee. I only made money if clients hired me. Going in to work on a Saturday didn't necessarily generate more income. Plus, every time I calculated the cost for a hired project, I realized that I could do these projects for about half of the cost of a professional bid. Plus, plus no one ever factors in taxes. If a project costs, let's say $10,000, and you are in a 25% tax bracket, you have to earn over $13,300 to end up with $10,000 to give someone for a project I could do myself for $3,000. Plus, I'd end up with new tools and knowledge I'd have for the next project! So, over and over again I jumped into learning new skills to save money. The home and all of its needs completely absorbed my energy and my life.

After reading one of the many self-help books that I mentioned, I set a goal to be financially independent by age forty. As I was approaching that birthday, I felt no closer to that goal than when I was twenty. As my lifestyle had creeped up, the cost to become financially independent had also risen by a huge factor.

Everyone I knew was in the same boat. Earning, buying, borrowing, working, spending for the right of a vacation or two a year and the dream of "being done" one day. Retiring. Then what? Travel a bit more if you're lucky, spend some time with the grandkids, and wait to die?

My stepdad had retired at age fifty-five. At that time, my sixteen-year-old brain wasn't impressed and didn't really take notice. Fifty-five was old to me, and I thought it was what he was supposed to do. He got a brain tumor at age seventy, and he was gone by seventy-two. Had he worked until normal retirement age he would've had about five years to live the way he'd always wanted to. Because of his planning and determination, he got to have many more years of that satisfying life away from a job that was stressful and no longer gratifying. As I approached my fortieth birthday, fifty-five didn't seem that far away, and I knew I wouldn't be free by then.

This began to hit me harder and harder. I would find myself leaning on a rake, daydreaming about being in college or traveling again . . . one day. *One day. One day, but not now. Back to work Carlo. There are chores to do, bills to pay. Back to work. If I just work hard enough, I can get ahead.*

And I did work. When I was twenty-four, I began my career as a financial planner and joined a firm that normally didn't hire advisors unless they were thirty and had meaningful connections. I obviously wasn't thirty, and I didn't grow up with wealthy connections. Using the information and motivation I got from the books I'd read, I pushed myself to learn the things I needed to learn. I convinced the manager of the company to give me a chance. I told him that before he hired me, I'd find clients first who wanted to work with me. I went back to my old bosses that I'd worked for in college and high school and talked to them. They agreed to become my clients, but I had no idea how to help them. Because I'd done a good job for them at $3.35—to eventually $6.00—per hour, they gave me a chance.

In 1996, I said goodbye to my last regular paycheck, agreed to get a draw of $2,000 per month for three months, which I would have to pay back. If I was earning money after three months, I could keep this job, but with no certain paycheck. I was like a hunter-gatherer, constantly searching for new clients and new people to help. I liked to help people, so this fit my natural strengths, and my fear of poverty drove me with a burning fire. I worked and worked and worked. Learning more, and eventually earning more. But it was never enough. Twenty years after I'd started, I was no more free than when I'd first walked in the door.

In fact, I felt less free because my list of wants was so big. I had so many things that had their own needs. Everything I owned, owned me. I spent thousands of dollars each year just cutting off branches from the ginormous oak trees that hovered over our home. I loved seeing the big trees, but man, they were a luxury! Each year a branch the size of a tree itself would die, and we'd have to hire folks with a cherry picker and tree climbing gear to safely remove it before it fell and punched a hole in the roof.

Everything I owned, owned me.

In addition, as a financial advisor, I was well aware of how much college was going to cost for my two sons. I was fortunate to be making more and more money, but I was less and less free. The things I owned and the life decisions I'd made were absorbing nearly everything I could earn. There was always another project. Another thing. And we weren't living a lavish lifestyle by any means. Like so many Americans, I would've described myself as being middle class, but the demands on my time and income made me feel constant anxiety about money, especially since I was self-employed.

By the time I was thirty, I'd left the company I'd started my career with and co-founded my own financial planning firm. This meant I now had payroll for staff, a lease, and countless other responsibilities and commitments with no guarantee of success. When you're growing a business, you're always trying to grow it not only for your own income, but you have to grow it enough to hire people, so you can do your profession.

Just work harder Carlo. Set bigger goals. Just work harder, and it will pay off.

I Was Only a Fancy Serf.

I love connecting to history and the lessons it can teach. When my boys and I were in Austria, we spent four nights in Salzburg.

Salzburg is one of those mountain towns in Europe that could be a set for a Disney movie. It is absolutely, perfectly adorable in so many ways—nestled in a mountain valley with the lovely Salzach river running through it, sitting in the shadow of the Hohensalzburg Fortress perched on a high point above the village.

One day we made our way up to the fortress for a tour. In one part, there's a mural with lots of information about the structure's one-thousand-year history. My boys and I read through it and were struck by how many times the fortress had been used as a safe haven for the wealthy when the serfs rebelled. Over and over again.

Back then, the wealthy lords owned all the land and the serfs who farmed it payed rent to live there. The rent was usually every-thing they grew with just enough to survive on themselves in a good year. They were tied to the lords in many ways and didn't have much of a path to freedom. They worked the land as their parents had and as their children would. As I read this history, I felt like our society had repackaged this same system in a way that gives the false impression that people today are free, that they aren't serfs at all.

Drive through any middle-class neighborhood full of giant American homes. The cars are parked in the driveway because the garage is full of stuff. The house is full of stuff, the basement is full of stuff, and sometimes there's is a storage unit somewhere that holds still more stuff. The house and the cars are on payment plans, and if there are children, there's not always a clear idea of how to fund their education, so they take advantage of financial aid packages from the colleges which adds more debt. As parents think about their kids' education needs, they remember that they're still paying for their own education—a decade or more after the fact. Every weekend they dig their outdoor tools out of the garage or shed and go to work to "farm" inedible plants they will pay to have taken away (think grass clippings). They send their money off to the banks, then run around town in the cars they co-own with the bank to buy more stuff. Yet, this is middle class. This is the American Dream, right? To have a house and a yard for barbeques, and maybe even a pool or hot tub (I had one of those too)!

How is this *not* serfdom? Since many people purchase these things on payment plans—including the college education they received years ago and the one their own kids are going to get—they are only owners as long as they keep making money and sending it to the bank. If there's a sickness, disability, death, lay-off, or any other disruption to the income, the lords will come and take their stuff back. The concept that we are an ownership society is a myth, and too many people are embarrassed to live within their means.

The American Dream that most people are living is simply a mortgage on their life. I'm not the first to point this out, but the word mortgage is a compound word made up of *mort* and *gage*—two old French words. Mort means death and gage means pledge. So, we work and work and work to pay off our death pledges to the lords. In this age of serial remodeling, refinancing, and relocating, most people continually start the death pledge over and over and over. Even when people save enough money to pay off their home and retire, the things they own still consume a great deal of their money, and more importantly, the precious minutes and hours of time they have left.

> ### *The American Dream that most people are living is simply a mortgage on their life.*

Only a small percentage are able to break out of that system. From the outside, you can't tell who they are. Books like *The Millionaire Next Door* highlight how many people who are wealthy and financially independent but don't live lavish lifestyles. Two neighbors with the same house and similar cars could have lives that look the same from the outside, but in reality, they could be very different. One person can afford it, and the other owns it all with the bank. It's a debt financed illusion of what my buddy called the "pre-rich". The pre-rich are happy to finance a lifestyle beyond where they are today because they are certain they'll be rich enough to pay for it one day. One day . . .

Complications

Horology is the art of making clocks and watches. In watchmaking, any feature beyond the hour and minute hands is considered a *complication*. A wristwatch can only be so big and remain practical. Adding a second hand requires more parts and pieces, gears, and springs that must all fit within roughly the same space as the hour and minute hands. Add a little window with the day of the week, and that's another complication. Add the month and there's another. Each complication requires more parts and pieces to work within the same tiny space. That pretty much exhausts my knowledge of watchmaking, but judging how expensive fancy Swiss watches can be—especially the ones with multiple complications—you can guess how difficult it must be to make all of that work in such a tiny space.

Your life is the same. You only have so much time and space. Even if you had unlimited money, you still only have so much time, and none of us know how much time we really do have. Everything you bring into your life takes time and money and adds complications. Having a home with a big yard meant that I was either a groundskeeper or I had to give my money away to hire one. The house, the yard, and all my stuff were complications that absorbed massive amounts of my time and my money, which had already absorbed my time to earn. Everything I owned was constantly pulling at my time and money, which was pulling me from what I really wanted to do with my time and life.

> ## Your life is the same. You only have so much time and space.

I use that watch metaphor whenever I'm making decisions about things I bring into my life, as well as relationships and other time commitments. I'm a single dad, a business owner, and an individual who's working on the things I love that make me feel like I'm growing and really living. I think hard about what and who I allow into my life that would affect this. That may sound harsh, but I once gave up a large part of my life to things that made me feel empty, and I will not go there again.

During the seven weeks that I lived with my brother at the beginning of my divorce process, I was sleeping on the leaky air mattress in what would one day be my nephews' bedroom. I'd lie there before and after sleep, trying to imagine what was next in my life. It was a scary, stressful time, to say the least.

One morning I was thinking about where I would live. My brain started scanning my existing neighborhood for homes that I might be able to afford. I imagined finding a smaller home. As my mind began forming an image of a home, I suddenly saw myself on a ladder cleaning the gutters of this new home that I didn't own yet.

Have you ever cleaned out a clogged gutter? When a gutter's clogged, it's full of the most foul-smelling, putrid water you can imagine and all kinds of organic matter that's been sitting and rotting in the gutter for weeks or months. So, you get out a big heavy ladder—because by default gutters are way up high on the roof—and you raise the extension ladder up to the appropriate level. Then you mess around with the footing to make sure it's level and secure, so it doesn't fall over when you are up high. Then you climb up the ladder, hoping this isn't going to end up on the evening news. Once you reach the top of the ladder, you get to fish out slimy bits of decomposed organic matter until the gutters can drain again while mosquitos swarm around you because you've disturbed their nesting ground! To make it worse, we'd had a two-story home with a walkout basement, so the gutters on the back of that house were really, really, really high.

As I laid there on the floor with this image, I had an extremely powerful reaction. I heard a loud "NO" in my mind. *No, I don't want gutters. I'm done with gutters. No, I don't want a lawn mower or a rake or any more of those things. I don't want to spend another weekend raking. I'm super done owning all of these things and having all of these jobs. I'm done losing nice weekends to yardwork that will have to be done again the following week. I'm done telling my kids that I can't spend time with them because I have to work on the house. I'm done giving away thousands of dollars over and over again to a never-ending list of projects, nor do I want to hire and manage a team of people to grow, mow, and then throw away grass clippings.* (For the record, I did compost my grass, but paying someone to do that would be even more expensive).

So, I decided to live in a condo, which is something I'd never done before. This decision gave me the time I needed to do so much of what I've been sharing with you. I needed the freedom to heal, learn, and grow. Sometimes I needed my weekends to do nothing, or go for walk, or take a drive, or take a class. I didn't want to mow and rake. The amount of time and energy I've wasted raking, mowing, fixing, painting, replacing, etc. is mind-numbing. I haven't mowed a lawn in over eight years now. I assume it's like riding a bike and that I could do it if I wanted to, but so far, the urge has not come over me.

The efficiencies of living in a multifamily building has freed me from so many expenses, too. Aside from not having to own, maintain, and use thousands of dollars of equipment to care for a home, there are some cost savings that are substantial that millions of Americans could benefit from.

For example, this year the association replaced the roof of our building. The cost for the project was $50,000. That sounds like a huge number until you compare it to a roof for a private home. I replaced the roof on my former house for $10,000. It was an asphalt shingle roof that had a ten-year life expectancy. The roof we put on our building is shared by twenty-seven families. The cost per family came to $1,852 for a roof with a twenty-year guarantee. So, the cost of this roof over a twenty-year time period saves each owner roughly $18,000! Paid for with after tax dollars to the real savings is $24,000 of pretax earnings using the same assumptions as I did above.

My condo is also much better insulated than my old home and has fewer exterior walls because I share two walls with neighbors. This means lower utility costs, around $200 per month savings. So now I'll save another $48,000 over the course of twenty years. (or $64,000 pretax)

These are the choices I made. I wanted to have time and money to focus on my growth. I wanted to massively restructure both to allow me to achieve the goals I have. Studying a language, art, and history takes time and energy, and it isn't something that's easy to do after spending eight hours in the yard. Hiring someone to do all that work is expensive and isn't something I wanted to invest in. I've gotten huge satisfaction from freeing up those expenses to get rid of my debt, to help my boys with their education, to build toward my own financial independence, and to have some real adventures along the way.

I'm old enough to know that I should never say never. I may own a home again one day. Maybe I'll have one in Italy with an olive tree, a fig tree, or a lemon tree and a view of the sea—that can be rented out when I'm not there. Who knows?

I know many people who dearly love their homes, who love caring for them, and their homes are a beautiful extension of what is them. If that's you, and you can afford it without stress or without feeling like you're putting the rest of your dreams on hold, then that's awesome. However, many Americans aren't in this situation. Many can't save for retirement, pay off their cars or student loans, can't help their kids with their education, can't travel, and can't do countless other things they say they want to do. Many more are a few paychecks away from bankruptcy. One trip to the ER away from financial ruin, but because of societal pressures, they feel they must have a certain kind and size of home.

If you feel like you just can't get ahead; you can't save for your big goals; you can't build enough investments to retire; you're perpetually busy doing things for your things and this doesn't light you up, then take an inventory. Think about how much time you have left. Create a list of the things you want to accomplish, places you want to see, people you'd like to help, and things you want to study and learn. Weigh out the consequences of not doing those things.

What if you found out you had a year to live? If the list of what you want to do and what you are doing don't match up, then think about how you can simplify your life. How you can be more free? If you're motivated to grow and learn but don't have the time and money, then take a step back and look at what's consuming your time and money, so you can begin exploring ways to free them for the things that will enrich you, rather than drain you.

> *If you feel like you just can't get ahead; you can't save for your big goals; you can't build enough investments to retire; you're perpetually busy doing things for your things and this doesn't light you up, then take an inventory.*

My process of restructuring isn't done. I'm having fun with it and am continually looking for ways to rethink how I spend my time and money. I know I wouldn't have made the progress I've made over the past eight years had I rebuilt the expensive, time-consuming life I had before.

Freedom is its own fun.

EPILOGUE

Experience is not what happens to a man; it is what a man does with what happens to him.

~ ALDOUS HUXLEY

A LOT HAS CHANGED SINCE I BEGAN this project nearly two years ago. I wrote the bulk of this book at a table in a lovely café just down the street from my home. I took great joy in strolling down there to let my thoughts dwell on whatever I wanted to say before I actually sat down to write. I enjoyed seeing familiar faces as I placed my order before finding my workspace for the morning. I loved the ritual of unpacking my laptop and my notebook with ideas I'd jotted down the previous day and putting on my headphones to listen to my music as I worked to get my stories out of my head. All of that feels like another lifetime as I sit here on my couch writing these last words.

It is August of 2020, and I haven't been to that café in six months. Like millions of others, I've been working from home since mid-March due to COVID-19. And there's no end in sight. I saw a comic in the *New Yorker* recently where a man said to a woman that he wasn't sure if he was working from home or living at work, and I can absolutely relate.

This grand timeout that we're dealing with in various ways has helped me focus even deeper on who I am and what I want.

The next steps of my life have become profoundly clear to me, and I find myself beginning many new projects on a life-altering scale similar to what I've already shared with you. These projects are new to me and too personal to share just yet, but I am excited to *yes and* them and to follow the fun and see where they go.

I'm grateful for the tools I learned in that winter of life that are helping me now. Because I learned to trust myself and love myself, I'm taking action quicker than I did the first time and doing so with more confidence.

In this time of pandemic, I'm grateful as always for having my boys in my life and seeing how well they've dealt with the switch to online learning and the difficulty of not socializing with friends the way they'd like. I'm also grateful for the tribe of friends, coaches, and teachers I've built over this last decade—people who reached out during the beginning weeks and months when we were all scared and didn't know what was going on.

Nearly a decade has gone by since I said the words out loud that had been echoing in my head: "Only ten more years." I feel like I've lived an entire lifetime since then, and I'm excited to see what each day brings in the years to come. I'm eager to dive deeper in my interests and curiosities. To see where they take me and who they bring into my life. Even in this strange time when I've barely left my home except to take walks, I've been diving into the things that light me up. I've read and studied more about the Italian artists such as Caravaggio, Titian, Giorgio Vasari, Raphael, Leonardo, Artemisia, and so many more. I'm making my way through biographies about Charles the Fifth and Charlemagne to better understand key points in European history. I started taking some German lessons to brush up on that rusty skill, only to be delighted with the compliments my teacher paid me about my grammar and accent.

Because of the things I've gone through and the lessons I've learned, I built habits and gathered tools that allow me to experience ongoing growth and mental stimulation without leaving my home. Of course, I want to adventure out, and when I can travel again I will, but the point is that I'm not waiting to be happy. I am happy. Now. I'm doing the things now. I don't need to check a box or get to a place to have the life I want. I'm living it now.

It can still be difficult. I haven't grown past being hurt or scared, but I have better tools to deal with life's challenges and to hopefully keep growing from and through them. I've circled back to nearly every tool I've mentioned in this book and learned even more. It's a process, right?

Your growth, development, and self-discovery are limitless. So, don't wait. Take that first step no matter how small. Say yes.

You can wake up to the dream inside that keeps whispering to you. You can be your own best friend, take care of yourself, love yourself, and watch how that love and growth spread through your life and to all those around you. Say yes, even if it's a small yes. Follow that which keeps tugging at you. Say yes to your dreams.

ACKNOWLEDGMENTS

THANK YOU TO MY SONS, Alex and Graham, for coming with me on this journey and for your love and support as I healed and learned.

Thank you to my amazing friend, Chelsea Ritter-Soronen, for your perpetual curiosity and enthusiasm for my dreams and passions and, of course, the memes. You continually inspire and amaze me.

Grazie a Valentina Colasuonno, my friend and Italian teacher for your help, patience, and support in my Italian journey. Learning about the language and culture of my roots brings me a joy I cannot put into words. You have helped me profoundly, and for that I am forever grateful.

I'm infinitely grateful for the life work and teachings of Ken Wilber, whose Integral Framework is ever present in my journey to grow up, clean up, wake up, and show up. Your writing continually stretches my mind and aids my growth and, like a compass, has pointed me in the direction of so many doors that opened to growth.

Thank you to my book coach and editor Nancy Erickson, who provided a process, the patience, and enthusiastic support to help pull this book out of my heart, so I could send it out to the world.

I could fill this page with the names of people who've been a part of my journey and helped me grow. I thank you all. I love you all and want you all to live your dreams. To live on purpose. To live out loud.

ABOUT THE AUTHOR

CARLO PIETRO SANFILIPPO is a Saint Louis native and a father of two sons. He has a passion for travel, language, art, culture, and history, and he's perpetually learning about these topics through books and experience. When he can't be in Italy among the olive trees, art, or ruins, he's transported there through the study of history.

He's worked professionally for twenty-five years as a financial planner, a career that's given him great insight into planning and pursuing dreams on many levels. Each family he's helped has given him another lifetime of lessons to learn and grow from, and he works hard to apply those lessons to his own life.